The Noticer's Guide to Living and Laughing

Change Your Life Without Changing Your Routine

MARGERY LEVEEN SHER

To Jennifer,
Happy Noticing!
Margery

Photo Credits

All interior photos are © Can Stock Photo Inc.

Cover design by Alexander Von Ness

Interior design by Kris Vetter

ISBN: 978-0-9908707-0-8 (Print)

ISBN: 978-0-9908707-2-2 (EPUB)

ISBN: 978-0-9908707-1-5 (MOBI)

The Did Ya Notice? Project™ LLC

www.DidYaNotice.com

Table of Contents

Preface

It's six-fifteen on a cold December evening, dark, but I am just beginning my "second shift."

I had rushed out of work, cursed the traffic, and arrived at the child care center to pick up my kids just before closing. Now one child is in the grocery cart, and one is helping me push. We rush around the store, picking up last minute items for dinner—chicken or hamburger? Crankiness flares and they require a pacifying snack. Fruit? No? Okay… crackers and juice.

Back at base, Jeremy splits off to the kitchen table with his homework, and Adam settles on the floor with his Legos. I stand at the stove, adding chili powder to the hamburger meat, answering questions, and listening to stories. My husband gets home and we all have dinner. More homework, play, laundry, and cleaning, before somewhat worrisome phone calls with parents who are getting older. Then bedtime rituals—and before you know it—the house is asleep.

The next morning, the whole routine begins again… and off we go. Off to the races!

I'm sure my life has been a lot like yours, right? Hustle and bustle? Good times with family we love, but a blur of speed in between?

Oh, I saw the self-help books; I heard the sermons and lectures. I'd love to take the time to meditate at the sea, and I do understand that there are more important things in life than money.

… but then again…

We have to eat, and pay our mortgage, and find the kids something to wear. So we need money. But really… we need something else too.

We need to *really live*—not just hustle and bustle. We need to appreciate what life has to offer.

And here's the thing: you don't need to get off the treadmill. *You don't have to change your routine to change your life.* In fact, you can *use* your regular routine to change your life. All you have to do is open your eyes and ears to what's right in front of you.

You just have to Notice.

Introduction

Let's get right down to it: Zippers! Broccoli! Ketchup vs Mustard!

Yes indeed. I am talking about the urgency of Noticing.

Noticing is mindfulness, with a smile. Being attentive to the world around you, and living in the moment. And it means seeing the pleasure and the humor that's right in front of your nose. Taking delight in Noticing what you see.

You see a zipper every day, don't you? You see it, but have you Noticed it? Have you Noticed what a simple, useful, efficacious and totally satisfying invention it is? Zip! You're done! A zipper is worthy of Noticing and worthy of great applause.

How about patterns in nature? Have you Noticed that there are patterns everywhere? Broccoli and cauliflower are among my favorites. A head of broccoli is made up of little heads of broccoli, which are made up of even littler heads of broccoli. Go get some broccoli and look. It's amazing! This isn't a 'ho hum' observation. A head of broccoli could have just as easily been made up of stalks and flowers going every which way, but it isn't. It's arranged in a beautiful repeating pattern. Notice!

What about the endearingly dumb things people do? Things I call, Human Idiosyn-Crazies™?

Do you ever try to listen to a traffic report only to find that before you know it, it's already over and you haven't heard a thing? Or perhaps you're a lousy, no-good cheater like me who makes a checklist, but then adds things that are already finished - to have the pleasure of crossing them off even retroactively?

Maybe you have strict rules about which sandwiches have ketchup, and which have mustard? Ketchup with chicken. Mustard with turkey. And no—do not speak to me of mayonnaise.

There are a kazillion things to Notice every day, but why is it important to Notice?

You want to squeeze everything you can out of your life, don't you? You don't want to let things slip through the hustle and bustle. You only live once, people—this is it!

Noticing doesn't take any more time, it is merely a mindset: a subtle yet vital mind shift. And you can share the Noticing mindset with your kids, your parents, your spouse, your friends, and your coworkers.

So notice what you see! You may laugh, you may cry, but I guarantee—you will get much more out of your life.

You don't have to change your daily routine. But if you use that routine to Notice, you will change your life.

This book is divided into the three categories of Noticing: Amazing, Annoying, and Human Idiosyn-Crazies™ to Notice. After each Noticing are suggestions for translating these types of ideas into conversations with family members or coworkers. You will become the hero of your office for Noticing patterns that will improve work processes. And you will never again wonder how to start a conversation with a four-year-old, a fifteen-year-old, or your eighty-year-old parent or grandparent. You will know how to Notice with anyone.

And most importantly... you will really live!

Vocabulary Alerts

- I have coined the term "Noticings" to mean each of my short essays on the things that have been Noticed. You can use this term when you Notice something you want to share, as in, "I just had an extraordinary Noticing!"

- Totally DeTestable Technology™ refers to what I, as Chief Noticing Officer, have dubbed as unnecessary inventions that usually don't work (automatic faucets, anyone?). Yes, these bring out my grumpiness.

- Human Idiosyn-Crazies™ mean the things we all do that are *endearingly dumb*. I usually advise a hearty laugh at these.

- Kumbayah and Un-kumbayah: Kumbayah is a Noticing that is just so sweet. Un-kumbayah is the opposite, Noticing something disturbing.

- "Radical Amazement" is a concept that was conceived by Rabbi Abraham Joshua Heschel (1907-1972). Heschel said, "Our goal should be to live life in radical amazement ... get up in the morning and look at the world in a way that takes nothing for granted. Everything is phenomenal; everything is incredible; never treat life casually. To be spiritual is to be amazed."

Conversation-Starters

You will find Conversation-Starters after each Noticing essay. These are suggestions for translating the ideas in the Noticing into conversations with family members or coworkers. You will be able to deal with work situations in a totally new way, and you will be able to engage anyone from preschoolers to grandparents in meaningful conversations (including even teenagers…maybe). You will learn how to Notice with anyone. And you will be laughing, and most importantly… and you will be really living!

Don't be limited to the Conversation-Starters that I suggest. Just because I suggest a way to talk with preschoolers, doesn't mean you couldn't use the same Noticing with another age group or even with colleagues at work. These Noticings can apply to everyone. Use them!

KVETCHES AND THANK YOUS

Ah, the life of a writer is a lonely one. The computer screen is an unfriendly companion, never participating, just silently reflecting back your own attempts. It never says, "Ha, ha. That was clever." Nor does it say, "Whoa. Better rewrite that gibberish." Begging it to say, "Yes! This is a future best seller!" simply does not work. It just sits there glowering, daring you to fill it up.

So thank goodness for my friends and family, and for my fellow Noticers who provide me feedback and praise. Thank you to everyone who subscribes to my weekly blog email, and everyone who reads my website. Thank you to everyone who has laughed at my Noticings. Thank you to everyone who has responded to my blog with cleverness of their own. Thank you to everyone who has clapped at my speeches. I love you, each and every one.

Special thanks to Sam Horn, who helped me discover that I am The Noticer. Thank you to Sally Strackbein for helping me formulate my Noticing keynote and my stories, and thank you to Cindy

Simons Bennett for her feedback and coaching on social media. Thank you to Natalie West, a most awesome editor. Thank you to Miral Sattar of BiblioCrunch, without whom this book would not have been thrust into the bookisphere.

Most special thanks to my Chief Operations Noticer, Stacey Minott Hardy, without whom absolutely nothing would get done. Very special thanks to my family for their incessant clapping (which I crave), especially my children, Jeremy and Adam and Megan (my spectacularly wonderful daughter-in-law). And most especially, thanks to my husband, Gerson Sher, who is my Chief Noticing Cheerleader.

I.

Amazing Things
to Notice

The number of Amazing Things to Notice is infinite. This section contains a sampling grouped into Amazing sub-categories. Actually, the way you can group and sub-group things is another Amazing Thing to Notice, but that's a Noticing for another day. For now, please enjoy...

1

Generally All-Around Amazing Things to Notice

Miracles

One description I could give about The Did Ya Notice? Project, is that it's all about Noticing miracles; those breathtaking little wonders that we see every day, but never Notice.

I looked up the etymology of "miracle" and learned that it comes from the Latin word miraculum, which means "object of wonder," and from the Greek word meidan, which means "to smile." I love this. By definition alone, there are miracles all around us to smile at!

We have been blessed with five senses with which to Notice miracles—sight, smell, hearing, touch, and taste.

Look at this sunrise. It's a miracle that happens every day, and every day, it looks slightly different. I had never before seen clouds that look like hundreds of little splotches of orangey-gold.

Think of your childhood. What do you smell? It's a miracle that the smell of something can bring back that entire phase of your life. When I smell chicken soup, or even imagine the smell, it takes me back to cozy suppers in the kitchen of my childhood home.

Unfortunately, I have little musical sense. But the adrenaline from sweating away as I listen to my favorite groups on the treadmill, carries over to my elevator ride back down to the lockers. Suddenly, I'm an elevator dancing queen! What's miraculous about that? Ha! Ask the person who found me singing and dancing my heart out when the doors opened. She's still laughing to this day.

Conversation-Starters with Preschoolers

Thinking about Miracles, you can start innumerable conversations with your preschoolers. Ask them to Notice five things around them that they can see from their chair while they are eating. Tiny things as well as big ones. Another time, ask them to Notice five things they can hear. As the week progresses, you can delve into things that they can feel, taste, and smell. The world is  constantly changing, and these conversations about using the different senses to Notice can go on indefinitely.

Conversation-Starter with Spouse, Partner, Significant other

Lots of times, we complain to those who are closest to us. We share our problems and our angst. How about making a deal with your closest friend, or spouse, or partner to share one "miracle" that you saw or heard each week?

Why do we have fingerprints? A recent study showed that the swirls and ridges enhance our sense of touch. A miraculous piece of engineering just by itself! We use them to feel our way through each and every day, and still, no one knows why each person's fingerprints are unique.

I am not a foodie. I do not like food for food's sake; I enjoy it for entire experience that surrounds it. Taste, to me, cannot be separated from the feelings I have when eating. After a fun dinner with friends, I will not remember the taste of the food, but I will remember the laughs and conversations we had. If I sneak an ice cream cone on a summer day, I'll probably forget the flavor, but I'll remember the feeling of wild abandon I'll get for indulging in such a wanton act. Moreover, there is nothing as relaxing and celebratory as having a cup of tea and a piece of pie at 4pm. Taste is warm feelings. It is memories. It is indispensable.

So to celebrate life's miracles, use your senses to Notice the world around you. You could very well discover an amazing new miracle!

Wise Old Aristotle

Aristotle once said, "The whole is greater than the sum of its parts."

This is true of the world. When I think about the parts of something coming together to make an amazing whole, I consider the result, the *gestalt* of something.

How often have you been someplace doing something, when you stopped for a moment and took a step back to think, *how great is this moment*? That moment defines the *gestalt*.

Recently, I was in an art museum, enjoying an exhibit of Braque still lifes. As I wandered the halls, I began to think how lovely it would be to spend an entire afternoon sitting amongst the art, reading a great book. The gestalt of that moment would be tremendously pleasant.

I have been lucky enough to have enjoyed concerts in some of the world's most beautiful cathedrals. While I must admit that I am tone deaf and most classical music puts me right to sleep (yes, I am a low-life), sitting in a cathedral with those majestic sounds echoing up around me produces an unforgettable gestalt.

Today, I took a walk to the farmers market in a summer rain. The sound of the raindrops on my umbrella as I walked past the glistening flower beds and exuberant trees, composed an almost perfect gestalt. A gestalt made even better on my walk back home as I sniffed my bunch of multi-colored, spring-scented flowers.

I love to look up when I'm walking in the city and notice the

Notice *gestalts* with your parents or grandparents. Try to come up with different examples or personal experiences about a time when the whole has been greater than the sum of its parts. Perhaps you'll find that just sitting around a cozy kitchen table, talking with loved ones over the sweet aroma of good coffee is a gestalt in and of itself.

BE A HERO AT WORK
CONVERSATION-STARTER

The *gestalt* at work is the very culture of the workplace. What is your workplace gestalt? What aspects of it should you call out for praise and maybe utilize further? What aspects would you want to change? How would you change it, taking into account financial and other realities? Often, good things are taken for granted, and negative things are obsessed about. Does your group do that? How can you build on the positives of your workplace? How can you make your workplace gestalt motivating to everyone?

modern architecture of a new building juxtaposed against a historic one. I think beautifully designed buildings, both old and modern, are awe-inspiring. I recently discovered an old red brick building on Connecticut Avenue and M Street in

Washington, DC. It was round and topped with a metal turret, like a part of a castle. And there against its side, was a huge modern office tower. Both buildings were set against a bright blue sky, and puffy white clouds were almost dancing on the tall building's rooftop. A beautiful, if incongruous, gestalt.

You see… paintings, books, cathedrals, concerts, markets, summer rain, flowers, architecture, and lush clouds are all wonderful things. But if you combine them in different permutations and combinations, the whole is even greater than the sum of the parts. If you take a moment to find them, it is truly amazing how many stupendous things there are in the world.

May you enjoy numerous, beautiful gestalts in your life.

Celebration

I am a huge believer in celebration. You too?

As we all know, life throws mud at us from time to time. But this just makes it all the more important to celebrate things that are good whenever we can.

I strongly believe in Noticing and celebrating the "small things." Things like the first warm sun of spring on your back as you walk down the street. Things like a tiny park hidden in the middle of a huge city. Things like the smells from a kitchen where someone is preparing the good stuff; sautéed onions, cinnamon breakfast rolls... a golden batch of chocolate chip cookies.

I also believe in parties. (Now this is beginning to sound like a strange religion... 'a believer in celebration and parties!') But I do love to throw parties. Of course there are the usual birthdays or Fourth of July weekends, but I think this year I will throw parties to celebrate coziness on a winter day, or the first flower of spring, or maybe even just a party to celebrate Tuesdays!

Tuesday is a nice day, and often neglected. People are always moaning about Monday, Wednesday gets the special name, Hump Day, Thursday begins the weekend celebration (at least if you are under thirty), and Friday gets to kick off the weekend. Only poor Tuesday is left out!

But Tuesday is a good solid day. By Tuesday, we're finished complaining about the work week starting, and we really buckle

Talk about the idea of making up celebrations, like celebrating Tuesday. What other celebrations would be good to have? Let your teen have these celebrations with friends (if they are reasonable...).

down. It's a day of accomplishment. It's a day of goals. We believe we can still accomplish a lot in the days to come. Tuesday is an optimistic day, and we should give it a party of its own!

So celebrate what strikes *you* as lovely. Celebrating the regular holidays is important, but celebrate other stuff too. Celebrate getting a bunch of stuff done! Celebrate being warm inside on a freezing cold day! Celebrate being outside on a beautiful warm day! Celebrate Noticing something new! Celebrate throughout the year.

Party hardy, as they say. Life is good and sweet, and when it's not, kick the bad in the butt with a party! Cheers!

Ice Cream Cones

You have to be happy when you eat an ice cream cone.

If you were sad, angry, or just feeling lethargic, you wouldn't want to eat an ice cream cone. It simply wouldn't appeal to you, would it?

Sometimes, if you're feeling a little wistful, an ice cream cone can cheer you right up. I often have a cone on the anniversary of my mother's death.

Now I don't often reveal my wild and crazy side to strangers... but I am ready to admit that I have a real chocolate cone once a year. Just to have it! Ha!

Ice cream cones define summer. I love summer and firmly believe we must hang onto the warm sunny days by our fingernails, until the cold blast of fall air brings us to our senses.

Happy chocolate chip! Happy rocky road! Happy strawberry swirl! In fact, happy plain old and still good, vanilla!

Oh, and by the way, there is absolutely no shame in biting off the cone's bottom and sucking the ice cream out that way. That's right Noticers—the truth is out now on this one!

Do ice cream cones make your child feel happy? What other foods make them happy? Hot dogs? Cupcakes? What would they like to eat when they are cold? Soup? Oatmeal? How about when they are sad? Is there a food that can cheer them up? Maybe a peanut butter and jelly sandwich with a smiley banana face on top? Are there foods that  are better in summer than winter? It's interesting that people who live in cold climates often eat ice cream in winter!

You can have many conversations about foods and the feelings they evoke. Although you should talk about not substituting eating for dealing with problems, I personally believe that a nice cup of tea can do wonders for the mood. And there is nothing wrong with celebrating a good grade by going out for ice cream!

Ah! The Wooden Screen Door!

There is nothing like an old-fashioned screen door framed in wood. They never seem to fully close, and they go clop, clop, clop in the summer breeze.

Maybe such a door is found only in the country. I remember when I was a child, I was sent to a summer camp in the Pennsylvania mountains. My friends and I were both somewhat brave and slightly naughty, and although forbidden to do so, we regularly snuck through the woods into town. This was a vitally important endeavor—because as soon as we emerged from the woods, we saw Abby's, the candy store with a wooden screen door.

After emptying our pockets of all the coins we had in exchange for bags full of heavenly goodies, we would sit on the steps in front of the store, and listen to the door open and close, open and close. After a while, we would come to our senses, and run all the way back through the woods in great fear of being caught red (licorice stick) handed.

All these years later, I can still imagine sitting on the front steps of the store with the old screen door clopping against the frame. The warm summer breeze served as a fine fan as I sat there, eating my treats, listening to the chirping crickets and the muted hum of conversation, as the screen door created a percussive rhythm to the country symphony around me.

(CONTINUED...)

Conversation-Starter with the Whole Family

The family can play listening games. Listen to the sounds in the house—the heat, the refrigerator, the washing machine, etc. Can you find a rhythm? Can you make music together listening to the rhythms of the house?

How about listening to the sounds outside? Can you hear birds, crickets, fire engines, cars, kids playing, the wind? Can you come back in and make music from what you heard? This is good for preschoolers and young elementary schoolers—one child can be the cricket, one the bird, one the wind, etc...

Conversation-Starter with Elders

The wooden screen door makes me think of lazy summer days in the country. Marcel Proust's Madeleine cookie famously brought back memories of the Sunday mornings of his childhood. Talk about what things bring back nostalgic memories for your parents, grandparents, or older friends.

Be a Hero at Work Conversation-Starter

How about this for a workplace party, retreat, or team building exercise: Can you and your team spend time listening to the sounds of the workplace and make a musical piece out of it? If you're in an office environment, you may hear the copier, computers, kitchen noises, footsteps—each different for different people.

Every so often in my reverie, someone would go in, and someone would go out. Eventually, the sun would sink, and the store would wind down.

But the beat of the country day continues in my mind.

Happy Birthday

Happy birthday to me. I am celebrating at the beach!

This is the second year I have come to the edge of the earth to celebrate my birthday. I know that some people don't like to celebrate their birthdays, but I do! After much soul-searching, I believe this birthday-celebrating need stems from the memory of years of ice cream cakes all mushed together into a cold and sweet mess in my mouth.

So at six o'clock in the morning, I walked down to the beach. Having a birthday in October gave me almost an hour to watch the sun god slowly lift the bright orange ball out of the depths of the ocean, and raise it triumphantly into the blue sky.

It's an awesome sight every single time! What a gift to start the day this way!

The sunrise is a big thing, but you know I believe strongly in the power of little things as well. Noticing little things brings meaning and happiness. I Noticed some awesome little things as I watched the sky turn colors.

After the waves receded, you could spot many little holes. I'm sure you have seen this. Just think of all the creatures that live beneath the sand. There must be an entire civilization down there. I know there are various types of crustaceans and a kind of harmless worm that love to live in the sand, but these must be just a couple of the many kinds of creatures in there.

Sometimes (often?) conversations with teens are difficult to have. Read this Noticing to them, and then ask them to think what they have learned in the past year or several years. Not school stuff, but life stuff.

They may prefer to write in a journal rather than talk with you. But this is an opportunity to spark their thinking.

And then I came upon the best Noticing of all. I found lots of tiny pieces of shells. No they weren't beautiful like some of the larger, whole shells you could find, with the lovely coloring and markings and gradations in their shells, but they were more interesting.

Think of their history, the stories they could tell. They have been broken apart by wild waves in a stormy ocean, but they have survived to tell the tale. These shell pieces are stories; they are survivors from rough seas. And today, they once again shine brightly in the sun, radiating light and happiness with the savvy understanding of life that only years can bring.

Yes, time brings both scrapes to the shell and stories to the heart. But as long as the sun god keeps raising up the orange ball, the sunlight will reflect that history and its inherent beauty.

Happy birthday to the seashells... and to me.

2

Amazing Nature Noticings

Cauliflower

Cauliflower is Amazing. Romanesco cauliflower is chartreuse, and the head is a spiral-shaped pyramid composed of spiral-shaped pyramids, and those pyramids are composed of spiral-shaped pyramids, and on and on. The self-replicating form is called a fractal. Broccoli is also made up of a self-replicating pattern.

I have learned that fractals can actually be found in many plants and animals. I give you the nautilus, a snowflake, Queen Anne's Lace, a peacock, and a pineapple.

I am absolutely radically amazed, aren't you?

Cauliflower hold some secret of the universe, of this I am sure!

Be a Hero at Work Conversation-Starter

While patterns that repeat and repeat (fractals) can be found everywhere in nature, there are also many patterns in the workplace. They have to do with processes and people. Here are some examples of workplace patterns:

- How meetings are held

- How projects are managed

- How individual team members behave in meetings

- How the kitchen never gets cleaned properly!

You must Notice patterns so that you can either *disrupt them if they are negative, or replicate them if they are positive.* So what are some patterns that you have Noticed at work? Should they be replicated or disrupted?

Hexagons

We talked about cauliflower, now I just must talk about snowflakes.

You have heard, I'm sure, that no two snowflakes are alike. It's hard to believe, but there is just a huge number of possible arrangements of snowflakes. The number of possibilities is... one followed by one hundred and fifty-eight zeroes. If you try to write that out, you will see that it is a very big number indeed!

But here's the thing that struck me. All snowflakes start out as hexagons!

Now why is that? Why hexagons?

Hexagons are awesome! And they are all over nature. A turtle's shell has hexagonal parts, a bee's honeycomb is made up of hexagons, and... ta da! A cloud formation in the shape of a hexagon was discovered over the north pole of Saturn! Solar system geometry!

CONVERSATION-STARTER WITH ELEMENTARY SCHOOLERS

Do some online research together and discover all the hexagons in nature, as well as hexagons in everyday life.

What A World This Is!

I decided to study biodiversity.

Well, *study* is a stretch, but I did spend a tiny bit of time looking at websites, and a lot of time thinking about how Amazing it all is.

Species diversity. Genetic diversity even within species. Ecosystem diversity—like the Pacific Northwest, the Florida Gulf, deserts, and rainforests. Also, coral reefs are an incredible ecosystem—more on that in a minute.

Biodiversity provides us a huge variety of foods and medicines. Ecosystems purify water, produce fertile soil, and moderate our weather. And trust me Noticers, these are just a few of the reasons why you should love them. But perhaps the greatest reasons you should love biodiversity is because of the mind-boggling beauty of this enormous array of beings.

When you think about biodiversity, you also have to be fascinated with how it all fits together and interacts. How the world is one, huge, incredible system. (A system that we humans can screw up royally, but today I write about Amazing stuff and will not be grumpy.)

I am particularly worried, however, about coral reefs. They're dying. Reefs are an ecosystem teeming with life forms, both plant and animal. A really tiny part of the ocean environment that contains twenty-five percent of all marine species! And if we're not careful, we could lose them.

Let's talk about the Challenger Deep. "Deeps" are what they call really, really deep places in the ocean. In the Challenger Deep's exploration, they found three types of organisms: sea cucumbers, giant single-celled creatures, and huge shrimp-life animals. And guess what?! These shrimpy things contain the exact same chemical that is now being tested for treating Alzheimers!

There are several deeps in the sea. In the Sirena Deep, microbes are layered on deep-sea rocks. What do they eat down there? There's not much food so many miles down. Well, it seems that water seeping through the rocks generates chemical reactions that produce methane and hydrogen, which the microbes eat. Kevin Hand, of the Jet Propulsion Laboratory, says that these exact kinds of reactions may be the basis of life on other planets!

What a weird and beautiful and awesome place this blue planet is!

Highs and Lows

Every morning (ok, ok, maybe not *every* morning, but still) when I am in the gym on the treadmill, I watch a television station from France called France 24. (Watch, rather than listen, since I have my ear buds blasting whatever will induce me to put one foot in front of the other as fast as I can.)

Anyway, I love France 24. It presents worldwide news with a European flavor. But what is the absolute best part of the show? The Weather Report! I can't help myself! I love it!

You fly over the world in a hovercraft or something like that, viewing the continents from just a bit above. A geography review of the entire world in a just few minutes?! (Yes, you must already have realized that I am a nerd, a geek, a dork... take your pick.) But as you circle the globe, you get to see the temperatures of various cities.

For example, today it is ten degrees in Melbourne, Anchorage, and Reykjavik! Three places that are thousands of miles apart! It's forty-two degrees in Abu Dhabi. (Now, of course, these temperatures are given in Celsius, and I have to get out my old slide rule to figure out what they are in Fahrenheit, but forty-two degrees is really hot, of that I am sure.)

Ok, Ok. I did the work for you. Ten degrees Celsius is fifty degrees Fahrenheit, and forty-two degrees Celsius is over one-hundred and seven. Yikes! Abu Dhabi is hot today!

- Start a dinner conversation ritual talking about the high and the low of each person's day.

- Take walks together looking for things high up and things low on the ground.

- Consider planning family vacations or outings to see things high (mountains) or low (take a hike through a forest and Notice what you can see on the forest floor).

Geography is really, really exciting! Take a look at a map, an atlas, or a globe. You can imagine a trip to anywhere!

I have to make sure you know one more amazing thing: the greatest high and the greatest low on earth. No, I'm not talking about drugs, nor about elemental issues like great love or tragic death.

I'm talking about geography! Mt. Everest in the Himalayas is the tallest mountain above sea level at 29,035 feet high. But if you think about a mountain that rises from the ocean floor, then you have Mauna Kea in Hawaii—the tallest mountain from base to summit at 32,000 feet, even though only 13,796 feet of it is above water. Now these are really highs!

But before your neck gets sore looking up so high, look down! The Challenger Deep in the Mariana Trench is the deepest point in the ocean. It has been measured at 35,760 feet down! So you can go down in the Earth farther than you can go up! Cool, huh?!

Continents, countries, cities, oceans, rivers, lakes, waterfalls, forests, deserts, mountains, ocean trenches. The highs and lows of geography!

Ya gotta admit—the Earth is truly, radically amazing!

The Ginkgo Tree's Lesson

I think a lot about the ginkgo tree. Don't you?

This is one heck of an amazing specimen. The most amazing thing about it is that this species of tree has no close living relatives. It's one of a kind! And even more amazing—it has been around for more than two-hundred and seventy million years!

This tree saw the Permian Era. The Permian Era was when all land was massed into one huge continent, Pangaea. That era ended in a catastrophic event that wiped out most life on the planet...but not the ginkgo!

The tree then saw the Jurassic period, when Pangaea rifted apart and dinosaurs roamed the earth. The tree saw the Cretaceous period, when Tyrannosaurus Rex was king. And it has seen all eras since. It survived the Ice Age. It even survived in Hiroshima after the bomb was dropped. It has withstood fires, and it is not susceptible to pest infestations. This tree is one tough cookie!

Today the ginkgo lines many city streets and brings shade and beauty to us humans.

It can live to three thousand years! Its leaves are distinctively fan-shaped, and when it's time for them to fall, they do so all together in one, short dump. Here one day—boom—gone the next!

The tree was first found in China, and Confucius is said to have spent hours reading and writing beneath it. You know that in many cultures, including Chinese, the old are traditionally venerated.

This Noticing just cries out for a conversation with a teenager. Do they agree that toughness, resilience, beauty, and giving back are what we should strive for? What do these words mean to you? What do they mean to your teen? For example, take beauty. Beauty to an adult  may refer to a beautiful heart or soul. Is the teen fixated on their face, or muscles, or weight? Are there other things that they believe they should strive for to have a full life?

Now, we are in a world that venerates the young and the new.

Perhaps we should attend to ancient Chinese culture. Perhaps we should pay more attention to what we can learn from older people, plants, and animals. We could listen to their stories. Old souls, mountains, rivers, and forests contain miraculous beauties, like the ginkgo tree, that hold much wisdom for us.

Professor Peter Crane of Yale wrote the book, Ginkgo, which he describes as a biography of a tree. In an interview with Yale *environment 360*, Professor Crane notes that a lesson of the gingko tree is that we should take the long view, as we think about our relationship to the natural world. We are not the center of the universe, he reminds us. Some organisms have been here for a really long time, and we have not.

But while we *are* here, we have a great blessing to Notice: the amazing ginkgo tree. The tree is tough, resilient, beautiful, and gives back to society. Now there's a lesson for living.

The Stars Are Yellow

I am lucky.

I have something we all need: A great friend who understands me intimately, and can anticipate my every wish. She has even enabled me to lose weight and stay in shape. I idolize her.

Who is this great friend? Why Pandora of course!

Without Pandora on my iPhone, I wouldn't be able to work out; I wouldn't sing and dance in the privacy of an empty elevator; I wouldn't pretend to be a chorus girl in front of my bathroom mirror. Not to mention, I get so happy when one of my favorite songs is played—which is often, of course, because my friend, Pandora, understands me so well.

This morning, thanks to Pandora, I belted out Coldplay's *Yellow*. Lucky for me, I was alone in the gym. I love this song and it got me thinking about colors.

Yellow means happiness to me. I have another Noticing about how a bunch of wild yellow flowers can make me smile a huge smile.

But what about other colors? Green means freshness; I can smell green. Blue exudes serenity; I feel zen around blue. Red connotes energy; I can see and even taste my life goals when I imagine I am surrounded by red. Teal is my favorite. Both fresh and serene. Black makes me feel sophisticated, of course, and even a little mysterious. However I just don't like orange, which I feel bad about because I love to eat oranges and don't want them to be insulted.

How about you? What do colors mean to you? Is there a color that soothes you? Energizes you? I think my color feelings are rather ordinary. Are yours different?

I read that bees can see ultraviolet light, so they would see different colors in a flower than we do. Which makes me think... what are the "real" colors of something? Do we see the "real" colors, or does a bee? What does "real" mean anyway?

And does it matter... *as long as the stars shine Yellow?*

Chief Noticing Officer Defends Defamed Blossom

I feel I must mount my white horse and save the day.

Clichés aside, I read a most astounding article in the newspaper, and I took it personally for a couple of reasons.

First, here was yet another example of what 'I know not.' I know not... a lot. I am constantly slapped in the face with a new fact, a new person, a new technological marvel that I have never heard of. And here was yet another slap.

Secondly, this was clearly a defamation of character of one who bothers no one, means no harm, and is generally bent on bringing happiness.

Yes... I am talking about the geranium!

I was astonished to read that geraniums are inferior flowers, despised by proper gardeners. I didn't know that! I feel so gauche. But I love them because they can be bright red and they run all over the place—over the side of the planter and down the wall. They're totally uninhibited! Isn't that how flowers should be?

In fact, I know little about flowers. I choose them by their color. I love yellow flowers! What is their genus? What is their phylum? I haven't the foggiest, and I don't really care. Yellow flowers flopping this way and that make me happy! Isn't that the purpose of flowers?

I have another Noticing about how I love my local farmers market.

Conversation-Starter with Preschoolers

Go to a nursery or florist. Look at all the flowers. Talk about the colors, how tall or short they are, how they smell, if they flop all over or stand up straight. Act out the flowers. (Really.) Pretend that you are geraniums flopping all over, sunflowers tall and opening wide, etc…

Conversation-Starter with Elementary Schoolers

Which flowers do they like best? Why? How do the different flowers make them feel? Boys too! There are flowers on knights' shields, most well-known is the fleur-de-lis. Do some web research with the kids.

I love the sights, and smells, and the people, and the dogs, and the excitement of seeing so much beauty. The farmers arrange their produce as carefully as an artist. But I think what I like best, is walking back home with my bunch of flowers. I always pick them out one by one, lots of yellow of course, but sometimes I mix in some red and orange, or even purple.

But what kinds of flowers do they sell, you ask? Happy kinds! Pretty kinds! Uninhibited kinds that flop all over! That is the family, the genus, the species. No, you're right. I don't have a degree in botany or horticulture. But I do have a degree in Noticing that yellow flowers make me happy and scarlet geraniums make me laugh.

How about you?

The Higgs Boson

I have spent a lot of time trying to figure out what the heck a Higgs Boson is.

Amazingly, scientists believe they have found it.

This is supposedly the particle that gave mass and energy to matter right after the Big Bang.

What does that mean? Wasn't the Big Bang itself just a huge burst of energy and mass? What did the Big Bang come from? And if the Big Bang began the universe, and the universe is a discernible entity, albeit an expanding one, what is outside the universe? How do we know there was only one Big Bang? Why couldn't there be multiple universes? Actually, scientists think there are...

There's a fun video on the Fermilab website about the Higgs Boson; a scientist is talking about it by describing a fish in water. Huh? Since I know nothing about physics, I am spectacularly clueless here. Are there physicists out there who can speak simple English and really explain this?

And is there a psychologist out there who can explain why I am getting my socks in a stew about the Higgs Boson instead of watching TV like a normal person?

Conversation-Starter with Teens

Read this Noticing with teenager. See if they will agree to do some research with you and try to all figure out this Higgs Boson thing together. There's a dinner conversation for you.

Cooperation, Persistence, and Fun

Pretentiously, I call myself a "flaneur."

That is, I walk around Noticing. Usually, I Notice what people are doing or saying. Sometimes, I Notice odd things happening, or natural beauty, or architecture, or street musicians.

Today, a beautiful spring day called me out to be a flaneur again.

But today, I Noticed something new.

I Noticed cooperation. I Noticed persistence. I Noticed fun.

I Noticed pigeons sharing a bagel, just like many of you probably do on a lazy weekend morning. But the amazing thing is that these pigeons were *taking turns*! They weren't pushing each other aside to get a good peck. No. One patiently waited for the other to walk away a bit, and then he began his pecking. When he moved away, another pigeon began pecking.

I spent a good many years of my life running preschools. We taught the toddlers to take turns with a toy, since they were really too young to get the concept of playing together and sharing. First one toddler could play for a while, then the other would get a turn. These pigeons were just like well-behaved toddlers! They were really cooperating, and as a result, each got his share of bagel until they were full.

Watching the pigeons and their bagel made me hungry. Lucky me - I found a terrific sandwich shop to get my lunch. And as I was

Conversation-Starter with Family

How can the family as a whole better balance persistence with fun? Does the family have enough fun together to satisfy each person? How could you have more fun together, without spending too much money?

Now, discuss why persistence is important! What would happen if everyone gave up quickly on a hard task? Who can give some examples of how they showed great persistence?

How about cooperation? Talk about how family members cooperate, either by working on a task together or by taking turns. What do you do well as far as cooperation and persistence go? Celebrate that!

munching my sandwich in front of the windowed wall, it was my great luck to get an amazing lesson in persistence. A bee started at the bottom of the window, and walked up, until at some point, he lost his footing and slid all the way back down. Now this Sisyphus-type character did not give up. He started climbing up the window again, and eventually slid back down. This went on time after time until my sandwich was gone and I had to leave. But I wished the bee well and hoped he finally reached his goal. He was nothing if not persistent.

We sometimes find ourselves wondering, what is the best way to get work done? Well if you have a team, cooperation is essential, is it not? We must learn from the pigeons. And if a task is difficult, we must be persistent. There was no throwing up legs in defeat for the bee, and there was no whining either. He *persisted*.

But while the pigeon and the bee teach us lessons in success, I then learned not to forget the enormous value of fun. In the spring sunshine, I found a beautiful dog playing Frisbee with his owner. I enjoyed taking his picture until he eventually fetched the Frisbee and brought it to me, dropping it at my feet. He would not move until I threw it for him, and from that moment on, I was his only fetch companion. "Forget about getting pictures for your writing," he said, "it's a beautiful day and you need to concentrate on having fun!"

Ok, Smart Doggy. You're right. Cooperation and persistence are all well and good, but the opportunity for fun time is not to be frittered away.

Random Thoughts

And now... a Noticing dedicated to purely random thoughts.

I think there is a force in the universe that wants us to be happy, at least some of the time. Why else would there be rainbows, fluffy clouds of all shapes, sweet-faced dogs, music that makes us dance, toddlers learning to walk, geraniums clambering all over, and sun-showers?

Astronomers have recently discovered two gigantic black holes in far-away galaxies. Each black hole is ten billion times the size of our sun. Other astronomers have discovered an earth-like planet circling another star; a planet with a temperature of seventy-two degrees. In other news, it's estimated that the number of stars in the universe is greater than the number of grains of sand on all the beaches on Earth. Does that make you feel as small and insignificant as an ant?

I know, I know, I've dissed ants. I understand that ants have a complex and highly evolved culture, and I should be more respectful of them. Many types of scientists have studied ants, from social biologists to computer scientists, and they've gained important knowledge from these petite, industrious creatures. I will therefore try to be more careful to acknowledge the contributions of all beings.

CONVERSATION-STARTER WITH PRESCHOOLERS

Help them think of things that make them happy. They may talk about a toy, but push them further. How about dogs? Cats? Music? (Play and dance!) Flowers? Swimming? Sand? Playgrounds? Riding in a grocery cart?

CONVERSATION-STARTER WITH ELEMENTARY SCHOOLERS

Do some research together on ants. Here's a good place to start:
Conversation-Starter With Teens

Look at the NASA website. The pictures are phenomenal. You can see galaxies and black holes! How do they imagine they will interact with space in different ways than previous generations? What things about space are most interesting and most compelling to them?

The Wondrous Number 60

Have you thought recently about the number 60?

What a number! And what a mystery! Why are there 60 minutes in an hour; 60 seconds in a minute?

Although I paid little attention in geometry class, I do remember that there are 60 minutes in a degree, and that each side of an equilateral triangle is 60 degrees. The oracle of our age, Wikipedia, tells me that in the United States, we measure electrical utility frequency as 60Hz.

The Babylonians had a sophisticated number system based on 60, and they got that idea from the Sumerians and the Akkadians. So this is an old, old idea.

Why did the Babylonians use 60? Well, all kinds of numbers can be divided evenly into 60: 1, 2, 3, 4, 5, 6, 10, 12, 15, 20, 30—so this makes it easy to measure fractions of the whole 60.

It's also believed the Babylonians counted the knuckles of their hand, using the thumb as the counter. If you do this, you see that you have 12 knuckles on each hand, and 5 hands makes 60, so it is an easy number to work with!

My research also tells me that a snowflake has six main arms that are 60 degrees apart! A honeycomb is a hexagon with outer angles of 60 degrees! Now we can't attribute these 60s to the Babylonians, can we?

Woo hoo! A mystery!

Don't you love the number 60, now?

Conversation-Starter with Elementary Schoolers

There are a number of baseball players and hockey players  who wore the number 60. Do some research and find out who they were.

There is a picture of what an artist imagined ancient Babylon looked like here: http://tinyurl.com/d8fh53z

Cole Porter Knew Bees Do It

For some reason, I vaguely remember biology class in the eighth grade. I remember memorizing this phylum and that phylum, and thinking how I was sure to ace the quiz. In case you don't remember... a phylum is a group of plants or animals that scientists have determined have things in common with each other. There are numerous phyla... but I am even boring myself here.

The point is, I find myself thinking again about bio-diversity. Why are there so many different kinds of species? Why is there such complexity?

Take, for example, honeybees and flowers.

I was driving on the NJ Turnpike recently in a light rain. Everything was gray, and the windshield wipers were rocking me to sleep. But by sheer luck, I was jolted awake by a news report on the enormity and complexity of our marvelous—and we must marvel—world.

I was lucky enough to be listening to Science Friday on NPR, and I learned some incredible things...

Guess what?! Flowers give off an electrical field to attract bees. Yes, they actually have electricity emanating from them! The bees are drawn in by the field because, evidently, they have a little charge themselves that is opposite to the flower's.

Yet, these wily flowers are even smarter than just being charged. They're caffeinated! Yes, a little bitter caffeine hides in their sweet nectar. Why?

It seems that the caffeine makes the bees a little more alert, so they'll remember the type of flower they're in. That way, when they fly off, they head towards another flower of the same type and begin to pollinate.

Way cool, huh?! A little bite with the sweet nectar. An electrical attraction. No wonder they call it the birds and the bees. Next I will have to see how birds do it. Do they also look for a cup of joe before they fly off to find a mate?

Wasn't I lucky to be jolted awake to learn about the honeybees and flowers? Maybe an electrical attraction from the bees came through the car radio to provide that jolt to awaken me. Maybe the coffee I am drinking now helps me remember my excitement so I can tell you all about the bees, and get you to pollinate another person's imagination with the wonders of our world!

Or alternatively, you could dance to *Birds Do It; Bees Do It*, and just marvel at the world.

Ducks

Early in the morning, I walked down to the river. It was a beautiful morning, and the light made the river shine. The current was calm, and slow ripples flowed gently by. I watched the ducks.

First I saw three in a row paddling along, one behind the other. They stopped to dip their beaks into the water and floated around in circles for a while. Then they paddled on again, except, the middle duck did not rejoin the others. 'Middle duck' stayed and dipped around the water looking for food, I guess.

Soon, two more ducks came paddling along, one behind the other. The middle duck from the first group paddled over to join them. "What about your other friends?" I said. "Don't you want to join them again?" No, I guess he didn't care about his old friends anymore.

He tried to join the other ducks by getting in front of them and leading the line. But the first duck gave him a loud quack. "And just who do you think you are, buddy?" he said. So the new duck got in the middle of the other two. Once a middle duck, always a middle duck.

I was surprised the last duck didn't want to move up and make the newcomer bring up the rear. Maybe 'last duck' had a poor self-concept and just thought of himself as always last. Or maybe 'last duck' had a great self-concept and thought of himself as the mighty and important caboose, and nobody was taking that away from him!

So all the ducks paddled on down the river. The first two far off in the distance, and the last three, including the duck who moved from one tribe to the other, just paddling along on a beautiful summer morning.

3

Amazing Noticings About the Seasons

Princess Summerfall Winterspring

I love Princess Summerfall Winterspring! She was a star of the Howdy Doody Show. This is worth a Google.

I love also how her name ends with a spring! Spring necessitates an exclamation point!

Spring is upward moving. Spring puts a hop in your step. Spring puts a smile on your face.

Imagine if her name had followed our calendar, and been Winter spring Summerfall—do you see how this would end in a downer? No, it follows the natural order instead and leaves us in *Spring*, a glorious new beginning! New plants, new animals, new energy.

Hooray for Spring! The name derives from the Old English word *springan*, which means to leap and burst forth. Don't you just want to leap when it is Spring?

Do you think I'm overly enthusiastic? Maybe, but I love spring! Flowers bloom. The sun shines with remembered warmth. People are out and about, enjoying what they enjoy outside. I Notice the freshness of the breeze, the colors all around, the simple contentment of people sitting outside.

How about you? What brings a spring to your step?

Thank you, Princess Summerfall Winterspring, for leaving us with a Spring!

Conversation-Starter with the Whole Family

Great dinner conversation—what season does each person like best? Why? What are the good things about each season? What are the negatives of each season? Who thinks the positives outweigh the negatives? Why? If one person just hates a season, have everyone come up with ways to make the

season seem better for that person. For example, if someone hates winter, promise to keep a comforter just for her on the sofa. If someone hates summer, promise to bring him a cold drink as he sits at his computer, at least once a week. Watch their negativity and grumpiness turn to smiles.

The Glory of the Seasons

I never eat fruit out of season. The glory of summer is manifest in its fruit.

If you could even get good tasting fruit out of season, eating it all the time would make it so much less special. It would be like people living forever. It sounds good, but by your 150th year, I bet it would become bland. Ho hum, another glorious sunrise peaking over the ocean's horizon. Ho hum, another tree coated with sparkling icicles dancing in the sun.

And so it is with grapes out of season. What is the smell of summer? I say it is the scent of fresh green grapes.

In winter, in the northern US, you can get grapes and even plums in your supermarket, but they smell like nothing and they taste like nothing. It is sacrilegious and against the laws of nature to eat fruits out of season.

Do you think that maybe I am getting too excited about your proclivity to eat grapes twelve months a year?

Conversation-Starter with Elementary Schoolers

What are the typical fruits of summer where you live? How about winter? What are fruits that are grown elsewhere in the world that you have never eaten? Do some research with the kids. I found ackee, rambutan, physalis, jabuticaba, and durian.

Conversation-Starter with Teens

Do some research about how fruit out of season arrives at our local grocery stores. Where is it picked? How is it transported? How nutritious is it when it reaches us? Is our buying fruits out of season essential to the economies of other areas of our country and the world? Am I selfish in suggesting that we not eat fruits out of season?

Wait! Wait! Stop! Please!
(A Lament for Summer)

It's eight-thirty in the evening… and it's *dark*!

Oh no! Summer, don't go! Please stop!

It was just yesterday, it seems, when it was light at nine at night, or even later.

I could get tons of stuff done after work—errands, walking around the city Noticing—and still get home before dark. But this not-so-slowly darkening of the sky, bodes chilly winds pushing me indoors for a hot cup of tea by five!

Summer, I love you! Red plums, green grapes, luscious sweet tomatoes, corn on the cob! The sun warming my back as I sit at an outdoor café. Baseball games! Barbecues! Riding the ferry down the river!

Summer: Wait!

Night sky: Brighten again!

Summer: *Don't go!*

Conversation-Starter with Elementary Schoolers

Talk about summer. What do they like best? What don't they like? Talk about the five senses. What are the sights of summer? What are  the sounds? What are the smells? What can they touch and feel in summer, but not in the other seasons? What are some tastes unique to summer?

4

Amazing Space Noticings

People! People!
We Are Talking Mars!

Robot machines investigating Mars, just think about it! This is really amazing, and I don't know why people on the street aren't talking about it every day! Earthlings have sent roving machines to Mars to explore. *Wow!*

The Mars rover, Curiosity, has bored holes into rocks and analyzed them. And what was found? There is now solid evidence that there was once water on Mars conducive to life!

Certain Martian rocks are made up of aluminum, silica, calcium and iron, just like rocks on Earth. Now you may say, "Of course. What's so special about that? We know what rocks are made of." But… we never knew what rocks on Mars were made of!

We could have found a mineral that we had never seen before. Maybe we still will. This is all awesome! And whenever we feel like it, we can see pictures of the Martian landscape on our computers! No, not an artist's rendition of what they think it might be like…

The real planet! We can see the real planet!

Sorry, people. I am just Radically Amazed at all this. Please be Amazed with me!

Conversation-Starter with the Whole Family

Gather round ye old computer and look at pictures of
Mars! Look at other
pictures from the
NASA website and
from Jet Propulsion
Lab website. You can
see all the planets
and more. Saturn
is awesome! Look for a picture of the hexagonal cloud over
Saturn's north pole!

Mars—Are New Silks and Spices in Our Future?

More Mars Amazement from me.

This is more than awesome! On NASA's website you can see real pictures of the surface of Mars, and you can see the Curiosity Rover tire tracks in Martian soil!

Holy Katoodles! Yowza!

I don't understand why people aren't excited about this all the time. What a feat! And what will be discovered? Please *Notice* this exploration going on.

Well, maybe it's not unusual that people generally don't pay attention until the results are proven to be hard-core fact.

Probably not too many people cared about that crazy Marco Polo, or Magellan, or Amerigo Vespucci. But when they saw gold, silk, and spices from far-off lands, they surely paid attention!

What will NASA's "spices" and "gold" be from this excursion?

Conversation-Starter with Elementary Schoolers

Talk about explorers. What astronauts' names do they know? What kinds of explorers were there in the past? Talk about famous early aviators, the pioneers who traveled west across America, the famous early explorers who are mentioned in this Noticing essay. What could propel some people to want to explore the unknown?

Conversation-Starter with the Whole Family

Do some research together and talk about what practical inventions have come from various explorations. I've learned about practical results coming from space exploration like GPS, weather forecasting, and implantable insulin pumps.

5

Amazing Invention Noticings

The Zipper

What do you think is the most amazing invention of all time? I believe it is the zipper. So simple! So satisfying! Zip! Zip! And it does the trick beautifully.

Zippers are so superior to their competition... the button. A zipped up jacket lets you be cozy and warm. No cold wind can get inside. There is no button-induced gap for sneaky air to shoot through. And a zipper is quick. Zip! You're done. As opposed to button one, then another, then another, etc...

Zip wins! I love zippers.

A zip is satisfying. A zip is secure. That is... as long as it doesn't break. Why are you looking down at your pants?

The zipper is simple and effective. What is your Workplace Zipper? What do you do at work, or see at work all the time, but don't Notice or discuss how simple and effective it is? The reason it's important to Notice your workplace "zipper" is that you might want to use it more and in other ways, as most times it's just taken for granted and not used to its greatest effect.

Here are some examples of elegant solutions—some "Workplace Zippers:"

- Minutes to a meeting. Minutes to meetings stop people from revisiting issues over and over, and hold people accountable. It's simple and it works.

- A template for a PowerPoint or a report presentation. If you have an agreed-upon template, everyone knows what is expected. Efficiency at its finest. Maybe you should develop more templates for your office. They would save lots of time.

- A clear subject line in an email. This elegant solution makes clear what's being discussed, and makes it easier to categorize and find later.

So what's your workplace zipper? What things are done all the time, but not really Noticed? If you Notice it, you can make sure it's used as much as possible, and in different ways.

Find Your Workplace Zipper!

Trash Cans

Now don't make fun of me. I know this is ridiculous. But I want to talk about a most miraculous invention…

… the trash can.

I love trash cans! Think of it—we have a place to toss things we don't want, while keeping the rest of the area neat and clean. If there were no trash cans, litter and garbage would just be all over. Life would be a miserable mess. With this terrific invention, neatness is possible.

I am enamored with the simplicity and beauty of the idea of the trash can. Who first came up with this idea? I'm sure cavemen must have had a special area for garbage, but when was something constructed to have in the home and carry outside to dump when full?

An invention that lasts to this day: simple, beautiful, useful, and needed!

CONVERSATION-STARTER WITH ELEMENTARY SCHOOLERS

Have your children find things around the house that are simple, beautiful, useful, and needed.

- Have your children find complicated gadgets or electronics, and ask them how they could get same result using simpler things. (a good dinner conversation)

- Tell them how you accomplished things before some electronics existed—before smartphones, iPad, HDTV. (a good dinner conversation, too)

My Love of Lettuce Spinners

You know that I profess great love for trash cans and zippers. I hope they will not fly into jealous rages, when I confess that I also have great love for a lettuce spinner.

You wash your lettuce and put it in the top compartment, cover it up, and crank the spinner.

Crank, crank, crank, faster and faster.

I ask you—what could be more fun?! Then, as the spinner slows down and finally stops, you open it and there's your lettuce, shining proudly, all clean and free from excess water. The slightly green-tinged water on the bottom part of the spinner is also proud of its job well done!

Great invention! No batteries, no chargers, no lasers, no nothin' newfangled!

I love you, lettuce spinner.

Be a Hero at Work Conversation-Starter

Think about zippers, trashcans, and lettuce spinners. Then think about the processes you use at work. Is there a simpler way to do things? Is there a simpler way to get information to people? Is there a simpler way to brainstorm solutions? Is there a simpler way to plan and execute projects? Is there a simpler way to evaluate the work produced? Don't be a Rube Goldberg; Be a Zipper!

(BTW, Google Rube Goldberg. He was a most interesting inventor... There's lots of stuff that you might find useful to make your point at work. Remember to laugh!)

Another Miracle Invention

It was a dark and stormy night.

Really, it was. A frigid rain was whipping everything in sight. Brrrr!

I was walking to the subway to get to an event, and as I slopped through puddles, I was thankful that I at least had on sensible shoes for this adventure. My umbrella kept getting turned inside out by the wet wind.

As I trudged on against the elements, I began to think....

What a wonderful invention is the *overcoat*!

Why it's right up there with the zipper, the trashcan, and the lettuce spinner!

I pulled my wool coat close around me as the wind howled. Sure the coat was getting wet, but it would dry out just fine. I did an accounting of my temperature. My face was frigid. My hands inside my gloves were cold. My feet in my clodhopper shoes were warm enough, but just the slightest bit damp. But the rest of me...? Warm and dry inside my overcoat!

Just think—a coat can get wet, a coat can get dirty. But if it does its duty properly, inside the coat you can still be warm and dry. You can even dare to wear elegant clothes! When you get to your destination, off comes the coat, and you appear butterfly-like from your cocoon, dry and stylish. (Or if you are a man, perhaps not butterfly-like, but still an eminence of elegance.)

Conversation-Starter with the Whole Family

What are some other wonderful inventions? The umbrella is another favorite of mine. What else is simple and useful, and hardly ever applauded? Elementary schoolers would get a laugh out of applauding loudly for the zipper, the trashcan, and whatever else they come up with. Teenagers; how many simple inventions do they appreciate that have nothing to do with electronics or media?

Overcoats are another of man's miracle inventions, worthy of accolades. Worthy of Notice!

The Miracle of the Newspaper

I love the newspaper. No, not reading online. Holding the paper while sitting in a big easy chair, or reading at the kitchen table during breakfast—those are the ways to go!

My Sunday paper is $2.50, and the weekday paper is $1.25. What a bargain! For less than the cost of a latte, you can soak up knowledge about a myriad of subjects. You can get your hackles up! You can laugh out loud! Here's what I learned in one day:

- The Scots are talking about independence from Great Britain. Surprisingly, Tartan pride aside, it has something to do with who controls the oil.

- Weather Underground is a website that provides weather forecasts by zip code. How the times change! I thought it was going to be an article about the 1969 birth of the leftist youth movement.

- Wealthier older people (I do not like the epithet, seniors) pay much more for Medicare than lower-income people. They do not get a free ride. As I get to be rich-and-famous (a noble goal), I will be glad to pay more.

- I have to admit, I love the crocs even more than pig. (See my Noticing, 'The Source of All Knowledge.')

- There are fruits you can get in Florida that I never heard of: chocolate pudding fruit, carambola, mamey, sapodilla, and jackfruit to name a few. Yum... well, maybe.

CONVERSATION-STARTER WITH THE WHOLE FAMILY

Give each family member a section of a print newspaper. Then let each person report on at least one thing they learned in that section. Talk about the benefits and drawbacks of reading the news in a print newspaper verses reading online.

CONVERSATION-STARTER WITH SPOUSE/PARTNER

Make it a point to read a section of the newspaper (even online, if you must), and tell each other about whatever interested you most in that section. This will get you talking about stuff that doesn't include chores, family, or work. Yea!

The only complaint I have about the newspaper is that I never have enough time to luxuriate wantonly amongst its treasures.

6

Amazing City Noticings
(and one for the country, too!)

My City is a Small Town

I love living in the city. The sights, the sounds! But perhaps the main reason I love it, is that it retains the elements of a small town.

I gossip with the owner of the cleaners across the street. If I have a lot to pick up, she'll accompany me back home, carrying a load of shirts. She just leaves her shop with a note on the counter that she will be right back.

She leaves the same note when she goes to walk her beautiful Golden Retriever, Lucy, in the park down the way. When not being walked, the dog always sits in the front of the shop, never losing hope that someone will toss her slimy old ball.

The woman at the cleaners, tells me that the woman at the flower shop next door, told her that the bellman at the hotel across the street wants to ask her out. She's intrigued but hesitant, and asks me my opinion. "Go for it, of course!" I advise.

The owner of the yogurt shop sees me coming, smiles, and makes my yogurt with blueberries and almonds before I even get to the door.

The manager at the salad shop asks me if I want 'the usual' as we talk about business. He tells me that his goal in life is to get me to eat a different salad, or maybe even a wrap. But he starts small, coaxing me towards a new salad dressing.

I smile at the wait staff at the sidewalk café next door, and they wave.

The hot dog stand vendor asks about my family, and she tells me about hers.

I often run into neighbors on the street, and we share the latest highs and lows.

Aren't these the same types of things touted as the benefits of small town living? My city is my beloved small town.

Why I Love the City—
Bagpipes and White Horses

Today I was strolling around, as is my wont, and heard in the distance the lugubrious tones of a bagpipe! I followed the sound, but strangely never found the bagpiper. It seemed to be continually out of reach. But that is the wont of a bagpipe, I think.

As I was returning from my meanderings, I came upon an even more unusual phenomenon. The sounds of drums echoed closer and closer, until I could see in the distance a group of colorfully dressed people led by a band of drums, and... could it be... a horse marching on the sidewalk?!

Yes, I came upon an Indian wedding party. The men in traditional dress marched first, followed by the groom, dressed so elegantly and seated upon a white horse draped in gold! Following the steed were the wedding guests. The bride was not among them, so I think this was the processional to meet her. How elegant! How romantic!

This is why I love the city.

In a one hour walk, I enjoyed bagpipes and a white horse draped in gold!

This is the stuff of dreams.

CONVERSATION-STARTER WITH ELEMENTARY SCHOOLERS

If you Google 'Indian wedding party with horse,' you will see
beautiful pictures. Do
some research together
on wedding traditions
in different countries.

You can also listen to
bagpipe music together
on YouTube.

Why I Love the City—
Drum Circles

I love to walk around the city, just Noticing. Today I walked about four miles. It was just plain lovely and just plain exciting.

In fact, strolling through pocket parks watching the flowers and the people, is euphoric.

I had a special treat today when I came across a drum circle! A *huge* drum circle—maybe thirty drummers playing the best music and rhythms! You could hear them for blocks, of course, and everywhere you looked, people were dancing!

A happiness-producing, dance-inducing, rhythm-introducing, perfect weekend afternoon.

Conversation-Starter with the Whole Family

Make a family drum circle using pots, pans, up-turned trash cans, and whatever else anyone can imagine.

Unique Personalities

I just returned from a visit to Manhattan, and it struck me how every city has its own unique personality.

I think of my home town of Washington, DC as a city of hidden beauty. Oh, of course everyone knows it's a beautiful city, with the Memorial Bridge spanning the flawless river that leads you to the Lincoln Memorial, with the Kennedy Center sparkling on your left, and the Washington Monument gleaming towards the right. All the monuments around the city and the Mall are quite outstanding.

But the beauty of Washington, in my mind, lies more in the hidden pocket parks and tucked-away architectural delights. My favorites are the terraced gardens behind the Old Stone House in Georgetown, the little park surrounding the statue of Gandhi off Massachusetts Avenue, and the Roman-like Spanish steps in Kalorama.

But back to my trip. We stayed in a hotel in New Jersey overlooking the Manhattan skyline, a narrow line of impressive and imposing skyscrapers. It just looks so narrow! *A city that is just a line.* You don't have a hint, by looking at the skyline, of the enormity of activity within. You couldn't guess the wide swath of humanity that bustles behind the horizon. Such incredible activity on that long, narrow island. New York is a city of secrets within that thin, narrow line.

Seattle is another favorite city of mine. In Seattle, you are constantly

awestruck. Everywhere you look, you see mountains, lakes, islands, the Sound. The city is comprised of and surrounded by water and volcanos. A city of cozy coffee bars and outdoor astonishment.

Of course, cities cannot be reduced to one sentence. They are complex beings full of human interest, and natural and man-made beauty. So with that caveat, and with great hubris, I will attempt to summarize each of my other favorites.

Boston is a city of meandering streets leading through the pages of an open-air history book.

San Francisco is a shimmering beauty of steep, steep hills forming memorable neighborhoods, all floating down to the shining Bay.

New Orleans is a leisurely, luxurious feast of elaborate dishes, exotic drinks, and exuberant music.

Let's go abroad...

Paris is a seat in an outdoor café to watch and admire people, sites, and the entire gestalt that is, and could only ever be, Paris.

Rome is surprise. You walk down a street only to stumble into an amazing mirage: an astonishing sculpture, or an imposing church with thousands of years of history.

Prague is music; music in majestic castles and exquisite churches.

Athens: a mess and a marvelous miracle.

How would you describe the personality of your favorite cities?

Nerviness and Caring:
Ya Gotta Love It!

"My God! You absolutely gobbled that down! You were starvin', huh?"

Who said that to whom? A mother to a child, half-scolding, half-proud of her good eater?

Nope. This was a waitress in a diner talking to her customer!

Of course this happened in my dear home state of New Jersey. Talk about reinforcing stereotypes! Can you imagine the wait staff leaning over a customer's plate and commenting on the speed of the person's eating?

Only in New Jersey. The people there continually display an endearing combination of nerviness and caring.

After my diner sojourn, I went to a gas station. New Jersey gas stations don't have self-service, and as the attendant filled my tank, I asked him why. He responded, in a stereotypical accent, "We got a lotta' old ladies here. They can't be pumpin' their own gas!"

Yup. New Jersey. Nerviness and caring. Ya gotta love it!

I spent a lot of time on the New Jersey Turnpike this fall, getting to and from different family events and holidays. The Turnpike certainly doesn't pass through the many beautiful parts of the state, but it does pass through New Jersey, and it does enable one to get off the road, make minor detours, and pick up a bit of nerviness along the way.

Ask your teen if they have noticed differences in the way people act in different places. How would they describe your own town or city? (Besides boring, of course.) How about how people behave in different environments? Do they behave differently if they are having dinner at a friend's house, rather than at home? How is behavior different in the school cafeteria? Why might this be true?

Remember this with teens: Even if you don't get a good conversation going, you've put some thoughts into their heads that they might think about on their own or with their friends.

Back in Washington, DC, where I have lived for a long time now, I just can't imagine anyone commenting on the speed of a person's eating. The wait staff here approach the tables gingerly so as not to disturb the deal-making and top secret government plans.

DC is very different from New Jersey. But while the people aren't *nervy*, they do care. You just need to make time to reach out and create those neighborly connections.

Walking the streets of DC always brings happy surprises.

Remember the time I saw a man dressed as a prince riding a white horse down the sidewalk? And today! Today I was thrilled to discover one of DC's best secrets: DC is really the North Pole! Some kind of CIA business, I'm sure. Why else would I run into a bevy of Santas sauntering down the avenue? (Well it was SantaCon, when tons of Santas do a bar crawl, but hey, let's keep the magic of Christmas alive, shall we?)

Cities are funny things. Take Seattle, for instance. Seattle is as different from New Jersey and Washington, DC as you can imagine. One year I hosted Thanksgiving dinner in Seattle, and I remember waiting for the butcher in the grocery store to locate the turkey I had ordered. He found it and lifted it over the counter to me. But before I could take it, a man rushed in front of me and grabbed it away!

The New Jersey in me came rushing forward. I was about to scream, "Hey! What the h*** do you think you're doing?!"

But fortunately, before the words could get out of my mouth, the man turned to me and said, "Where is your cart, ma'am? This is too heavy for you to carry."

Ah, Seattle. How is it they are so laid back and helpful, while tanked up on gallons of coffee?

I love the unique personalities of different places, whether it's nervy waitresses, happy Santas, or latte-laden ambassadors of good will.

An Incredible Time Machine

I love maps. Not regular, ordinary maps that tell you where a road is on the other side of the county. No, I love maps that transport you back to a place you loved. A map can be an incredible time machine.

I open my revered map of Paris, and *voila*, I was back!

Look—*oh look!* This is the exact corner of my favorite bakery—Rue des Quatre Vents and Rue de Gregoire de Tours! I can almost taste the éclair! And then, if you walk up Rue de Seine, all of a sudden you come to the square with the St. Sulpice church! You won't believe it. It's an absolute sensation, and it appears out of nowhere in the middle of the neighborhood.

I can see where I would walk down the stately Rue de Varenne until I reached the gardens of the Rodin Museum. There I'd sit among the sculptures, marveling at my luck just to be there.

The map takes me back in time to serene walks in the beauty that is only Paris; the taste of pastries, cheese, baguette, crepes, ice cream in summer, chestnuts in winter. Strolls through beautiful avenues and stunning parks, the Seine and the cathedrals.

My map of Paris is my Proustian Madeleine.* I can see the golden leaves touching the blue sky, and I am there, smiling.

*In 1913, Marcel Proust wrote about the flood of memories that biting into a Madeleine cookie brought back to him.

Conversation-Starter with Family

Look at maps of places where you have taken family vacations. Have you been to the beach together, to the mountains, to  Disney World, etc...? Try to remember as many places as you can in that vacation setting. Where did you buy groceries? Where did you have ice cream or hot chocolate? Where was the museum and what did you see inside it? If you don't have a map of your vacation place, you can draw one together.

The Farmers Market

In my neighborhood, the Farmers Market on Sundays is the highlight of the week! Streets are closed and a bank parking lot is transformed to accommodate the spectacle. The white tents of the vendors can be seen from blocks away, luring visitors like a mirage in the desert.

You can hear the sounds of musicians as you approach. Music is interspersed with the calls of homeless men selling their newspapers, and barking dogs as they scamper around playing with each other on the grassy rise at the edge of the market. Their coffee-drinking owners chat with each other while they keep a patient and forbearing eye on their pets. The market is alive with people, pets, and produce!

I wander up and down the rows of vendors admiring the fruits, vegetables, yogurt, meat, eggs, mushrooms, soaps, yarn, and seafood until my nose leads me to the huge bakery. *Yum*! How beautiful the pastries are; how luscious the breads look; how overwhelming are the pies! I use all my internal powers to tear away from the magnetized oatmeal and chocolate cookies, and I am rewarded.

Rewarded by even more happiness… because here live the flowers! Beautiful yellows, and pinks, and purples, and orange! I always add a stalk or two of fresh mint to my flowers. Breathe in the minty sweetness!

I talk to the newspaper vendor while I buy one. He proudly

Conversation-Starter with Preschoolers

Take your child to a farmers market, or a farm, or even the grocery store. Talk about all the fruits and vegetables—their names, their color, their shape, what they taste like. Taste some. Smell some. Feel some. Describe what you taste, smell, and feel.

Conversation-Starter with the Whole Family

Go to a farmers market. Agree to buy something that you have never tasted before. Each person could select one thing. Then go home and enjoy (or not) the new taste together.

shows me the article he wrote about his fellow patrons of the homeless shelter. He's had it tough, but he is talented, interested, and interesting.

I watch the people. Couples holding hands, parents pushing strollers, students planning their day, and old friends meeting and leaving for coffee. Everyone admiring the beautiful produce, the savory empanadas, the silky tofu dessert.

It's funny. How can you be in the middle of so much activity—an avalanche of sights, sounds, and smells, and end up feeling blissfully at peace?

A Most Delightful Exclamation Point

A truly wonderful thing happened to me this morning!

As I was walking home from my beloved farmers market with tomatoes, basil, peaches, and my happy yellow flowers in my arms, an exclamation point bounced down upon my nose.

An exclamation point to my excellent morning, that is.

I was walking down a residential street in the city. Beautiful old townhouses lined the sidewalks, and on this particular street, the townhouses were set back and lovely gardens filled the spaces between the front doors and the sidewalk.

As I ambled along, I heard a voice, "Would you like some rosemary?"

I looked up to find a woman holding huge scissors near a bountiful bush. Would I ever! As I thanked her and climbed the stairs to receive this surprise, her beautiful retriever opened his eyes for just a second before drifting off again.

Rosemary was the perfect addition to the scent of the basil and the perfume of the flowers.

Another secret of city living: people are kind, dogs are sleepy, and the markets with their displays of fresh fruit, vegetables, herbs, and flowers are the finest art there is.

Maybe they never thought of it this way before but… can they think of a time that a punctuation mark "bounced down upon their nose?" Maybe they were quite sure about something, but then they learned something new, or someone said something that made a question mark

"bounce down upon their nose?" Maybe they felt finality about something and a period "bounced down." Or maybe something really great happened and they felt an exclamation point "bouncing up and down on their nose."

I'm Just a Country Girl at Heart

You know that I live in the city and love it. However, if you read 'Ah, The Wooden Screen Door,' you might have guessed that I have another side.

Yes, yes... I also have a soft spot in my heart for the country. In the last few years, I have spent a bit of time in the New England Berkshires—the lovely Berkshires.

The winding country roads, the hills and dales, the mountains. (Yes, I know they are only East Coast mountains, but they are nonetheless lovely.) There are cows grazing on the hillocks, horses and pigs. Farmlands are open for fruit-picking and vegetable-foraging. Even I, the ultimate city-slicker, was drawn by the sweet scent of freshness to sit upon the ground among the vines, and pick strawberries.

Surprises await you in the country. Where do you think I found the most interesting library? Why inside a butcher shop, of course!

The country is a special place that composes itself of a central green, a white church surrounded by little shops, a cozy library, and numerous places to sit and sip. All around are the barns and silos, the cows and the berries, the hills and the rivers, and a breeze that blows your hair.

It is a very special place, the country.

CONVERSATION-STARTER WITH FAMILY

Do you live in the country, the city, or the suburbs? Take a trip to the country if you have not been there, or to the city if that is new. Talk about the things that are different from your home area. What is similar? If trips are not possible, use books and websites as a basis for discussion.

CONVERSATION-STARTER WITH TEENS

Teens can Notice the types of music created by country artists and the types created by musicians from the city. Has one genre of music influenced the other?

7

Amazing Noticings about Knowledge or Lack Thereof

A Book Worthy of
Radical Amazement

Recently my husband and I were visiting our children in the country. We stayed in a lovely inn which had a sitting room lined with bookshelves, as country inns often do. There were books on music history, Shakespeare, luxurious cars (Ferrari even had a book of its own), novels, books about New England, and much more.

But the absolutely most fabulous find was a book of *everything*! *The New York Times Guide to Essential Knowledge. A Desk Reference for the Curious Mind*. Wow!

This was like finding gold in a rushing river! This is the book for us, Noticers! You have to have a curious mind to be a Noticer.

This book has over thirteen-hundred pages of information! Where to start? An interesting question in and of itself.

It's arranged into major categories with sub-categories within. The fine arts, the performing arts, science and technology, social sciences—philosophy, religions, and mythology—economics and business, media, sports, and food. There's also a reference library. Can you believe it?! This book is worthy of radical amazement!

But I found myself thinking, have they left any categories out? What else could there be? Are these the categories of *everything*?

Anyway, I really couldn't wait to dive in. Do you go first to the sections about stuff you already know about and see how the

Why not choose a specific time in the week for a half hour of online encyclopedia browsing together? Maybe Sunday evenings at eight, you all go online to an encyclopedia and see what you can learn in thirty minutes.  Maybe the kids will even ask for more time!

subject is treated? Or do you go first to something about which you know nothing? Or do you simply start at page one and proceed through all the way to the end?! Your choices will surely reveal something important about yourself.

I decided to start with languages, something that has always interested me. *Languages of the World* is in the social sciences section. It talks about language families (five major ones, and then sub-families), and a theory of where spoken language began (southern Africa).

From there I went to geography—also a fascinating topic. And finally, in this first sitting, I turned the pages until I got to a topic that completely dumbfounds me—mathematics.

This book is the perfect bible for a dilettante like me!

The Clovis People and
the Younger Dryas

The world has done it again! It has clonked me on the head and made me realize how radically Amazing it is—and how much there is always to learn.

I just read an amazing article in the newspaper about nanodiamonds found in Arizona. It relates how nanodiamonds might answer the riddle of what happened to the Clovis People and the megafauna, and why the climate changed at the beginning of the Younger Dryas!

Why do I not know anything about the Clovis except their name? Why do I not know what fauna were the megafauna of that time? And how, in all my long-born days, have I never heard about Younger Dryas? It seems I've found some research projects for myself.

Ah, Louis Armstrong was so right—it's such a wonderful world. You never know when some intriguing fact or idea will come your way, and a whole new aspect of the universe will open up for you. How cool is that?!

CONVERSATION-STARTER WITH ELEMENTARY SCHOOLERS

History.com has a great video about the origins of the Clovis people.

Physics: Amazing, Just Amazing!

I made a grievous error when I was in the eleventh grade.

I decided not to take physics since it had a reputation as being difficult and tedious. Instead, I took "general science." A class so vacuous and simple that I spent my time writing spectacularly clever and humorous notes (or so I thought) to my boyfriend.

No person in authority ever questioned my choice since I was a sweet and typical teenage girl, who blended into a sea of sweet and typical teenage girls, and society claimed such girls had no reason to study physics.

Now, all these years later, I spend much time wondering at how things work, and why I don't know anything at all about the essence of the world. It's like admiring the beauty of an intricately carved antique clock, but being clueless about the workings behind its face.

Well, actually... I am as clueless about the workings of a clock as I am about the workings of the universe. (Sigh).

Remember *The New York Times Guide to Essential Knowledge* which I first saw in the library of a lovely country inn? Of course, I turned to this amazing book to learn all about physics. I was excited! Finally I would correct my eleventh grade folly!

I read all the basic laws of physics. I read about mass, and motion, and momentum. I studied the formulas. I paid attention to what Newton, and Einstein, and Heisenberg, and Pauli, and Higgs discovered or theorized.

What does your teenager think of this Noticing? Discuss their criteria as they select classes. An easy A? Colleges' expectations? Personal interest? Discuss the tradeoffs when selecting one class over another.

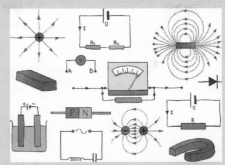

And I don't understand a word of it.

Perhaps I should give up on physics and just write clever and humorous (or so I think) notes to you, my fellow Noticers.

Or perhaps not.

I've written about the Higgs Boson and other scientific marvels. Perhaps one day I will figure out what the scientists are saying. Sometimes I think about it in the middle of the night.

Don't you? Doesn't everyone?

Are You Bored?

What?! That's *ridiculous*! Yes—I am judgmental! Open your eyes and look! Take a deep breath and smell! Taste something new! Listen, what do you hear? Feel something different! Think about stuff.

Why does the Leaning Tower of Pisa lean? Why doesn't it fall over?

Do you know all the things Leonardo Da Vinci did?

Have you ever looked at pond or creek water under a microscope?

What exactly happens to make cumulus clouds, verses cirrus clouds, verses stratus clouds?

Have you looked at the pictures on the NASA website?

Have you taken a walk at six-thirty in the morning? What are people doing?

How many sunrises have you seen? Where? How many sunsets?

Have you climbed in the mountains?

What have you found digging in the sand by the sea?

What smell is better than a pine forest after a rain?

Have you walked in the rain and loved it?

Have you watched a bee pollinate a flower?

What can you add to this list?

Conversation-Starter with Family

Do all these things listed, and add as many more things as you can!

8

Amazing Art Noticings

I Am A Know-Nothing; Can I Be An Art Critic Anyway?

I love Kandinsky's "Succession," an abstract masterpiece that makes me tremendously happy. It looks like the brightly colored forms are dancing across the canvas. It makes me want to dance! It makes me want to sing the notes of the painting. Maybe it's telling us how the world progresses. It's got to be a happy ending if the painted succession is so happy. We need happiness and optimism desperately these days, and well—there's some right in this painting.

At least, that's what know-nothing-me thinks. Am I allowed to express my know-nothing opinion, or will some real art critic tell me to shut up? A little intimidated, I did some almighty Google research. I learned bits and pieces like: Kandinsky considered his colors to be like notes of music. The forms he used are called "biomorphic" when they aren't geometric. He was also said to have painted his "inner necessity."

A little knowledge is a dangerous thing... I may have heard that a time or two.

Is it our job as viewers to understand what the artist was trying to say, or to just to react to it emotionally and personally? Both, probably. But as far as this painting is concerned, I may not know what Kandinsky is saying, but I do know that the painting makes me happy... and that's a good thing.

So sayeth I, Chief Noticing Officer and Art Critic.

CONVERSATION-STARTER WITH FAMILY

Look at pictures of Kandinsky's work. (Or see it in a museum,

if you are lucky enough to be able to do that.) How do the different pictures make each person feel? Who likes the art? Why? Who doesn't? Why? Elementary school kids might like to try drawing in the Kandinsky style.

You can, of course, do these exercises with any artist's work.

Art—Renoir

You know I love Kandinsky—happy symbols chasing each other across the canvas…

But my true confession is this: I adore *Luncheon of the Boating Party* by Renoir. I could stare at it for hours. It looks like a perfect afternoon—beautiful scenery, delicious food and drink, great conversation with friends. And a lot of flirting!

On the technical side, I'm amazed at how Renoir managed to convey all that reflected light. But most of all… I want to be at that party!

Do you know the movie, Midnight in Paris? People are transported back to any era they wish to be part of. I would insist on being transported right into that painting. A lovely Sunday afternoon with friends… and I think there is some wine left in the bottles for me to join right in.

"Bonjour, mes amis. I am delighted to join you!"

Conversation-Starter with Elementary Schoolers

Have the kids look at this painting on the web or in a book, and then ask them to write a story about the characters in the picture. What they are doing, what they are saying?

The Art Museum

How very lucky I am to be able to walk down the street and surround myself with fascinating, mysterious, uplifting, thought-provoking, awe-inspiring, joy-producing… art!

Art produces energy of its own, contagious energy. Art pokes you to remind you that you are alive. In case you are becoming complacent, it makes you smile, feel joy, or half-peer in disgust. It slows you down and insists on patience; it lifts you up ever higher. It amazes you.

Abstract still-lifes are among my favorites—Braque's, Matisse's, Picasso's. So clever, so charming. So much to *Notice*!

Conversation-Starter with Teens

Encourage your teenager to go to an art museum, look at a book of art, or look at art online. Ask them if they agree with my artistic assessment. Does art have contagious energy? Does it poke you? Which paintings make them smile? Have they found a painting that they half-peer at in disgust?

Conversation-Starter with Spouse/Partner/ Friend

Go to a museum together. Discuss how a painting or sculpture makes you feel. Not if you like it; not what it's about; not the technical prowess of the artist. Simply discuss how it makes you feel.

9

Amazing Noticings—
First Lines of Books

Let Us Describe Our Life
Only in the Superlative

As you know, sometimes I write about my radical amazement at things in the natural world. But here is another venue for radical amazement—the written word! I find myself mesmerized by the opening lines of great books.

Consider this:

> *It was the best of times, it was the worst of times. It was the age of wisdom, it was the age of foolishness. It was the epoch of belief, it was the epoch of incredulity. It was the season of Light, it was the season of Darkness, It was the spring of hope, it was the winter of despair. We had everything before us, we had nothing before us, We were all going direct to Heaven, we were all going direct the other way—in short, the period was so far like the present period, that some of its noisiest authorities, insisted on its being received, for good or for evil, in the superlative degree of comparison only.*

Is that not fabulous?! Imagine beginning a book that way! It makes me smile every time I read it! I wish I could befriend Charles Dickens. I'm sure he and I would have great fun roaming around London.... or maybe I would just sit star-struck and gaga-eyed at his feet all day. I have quoted, of course, the opening of *A Tale of Two Cities*.

Conversation-Starter with Family

Have each person read the first line of a book they like.

Charles Dickens.

(Even the toddlers can bring a book to the table!) Perhaps the elementary schoolers and teens would like to take a stab at writing a better opening to a book they have read. What is their favorite book? Do they think it opens well? How could the opening be different?

Spouse/Partner/Friend Conversation-Starter

What do you think of Dickens' opening? Can you say the same thing today? Do you find it comforting or depressing? Why?

First Lines—Tea

Under certain circumstances there are few hours in life more agreeable than the hour dedicated to the ceremony known as afternoon tea.

This is the opening of *The Portrait of a Lady* by Henry James. It so makes me wish I were a rich Englishwoman in the 1860s!

Perhaps we Type-A Americans should reconsider this ritual. Would it be so awful to cease and desist at four o'clock every day and have a cup of tea in a fine china cup? Perhaps a smidgen of crumpet?

I would guess that in Merry Olde England, certain gentlemen urged to join in this ritual, might have, from time to time, surreptitiously whisked out their tiny but potent little embroidered leather flasks, and enhanced the tea for themselves and the lady.

Then perhaps, the five o'clock hour became a spot more interesting…

Conversation-Starter with Teens

What does your teen think about this ritual? Yes, it would be impossible in America today with after school sports, clubs, and events—but what are the benefits of an afternoon tea ritual? Is there something else we could do to serve the same purpose  that would fit better into our modern lives?

Conversation-Starter with Family

Some day when your whole family is snowed in, prepare an old fashioned tea service together. Make scones or crumpets (even toast and jam will do) to have with your tea, and be ever so proper as you partake of this feast. Assure the boys that gentlemen, indeed, joined in this ritual.

First Lines—Children's Books

I love good children's books, especially books written for preschoolers and early elementary grades. One of my favorites is *The Tale of Mr. Jeremy Fisher* by Beatrix Potter. It begins:

> *Once upon a time there was a frog called Mr. Jeremy Fisher; he lived in a little damp house amongst the buttercups at the edge of a pond.*

This is a delightful beginning. You know from this sentence that Mr. Jeremy is quite proper and that his home, though small, was well placed amongst lovely flowers. You surely want to know some of Mr. Jeremy's adventures…

We soon learn that Mr. Jeremy liked getting his feet wet, and nobody scolded him about it. Furthermore, he never caught cold. Imagine the delight of generations of children in learning this fact. Someone can splash in puddles with impunity!

Beatrix Potter, of course, is also well-known for *The Tale of Peter Rabbit*. It famously begins:

> *Once upon a time there were four little Rabbits and their names were—Flopsy, Mopsy, Cotton-Tail, and Peter.*

You know right away, from this beginning, that Peter is different, don't you? And different he is. Peter has been our mischievous but loveable rabbit for over a hundred years. You cannot help but desperately root for him to escape from Mr. McGregor!

Great children's books have all the suspense, tension, humor, and display of human foibles as adult fiction. Good children's book authors do not write condescendingly to children, but rather lift them up with complex themes and emotions, enhanced by the vocabulary used. After reading *Mr. Jeremy Fisher*, no child could forget what a macintosh and galoshes are!

But the stories are short and therefore hard to write. Blaise Pascal, the 17th century mathematician made this often-quoted statement:

> *I have only made this letter longer because I have not had the time to make it shorter.*

So what is amazing and worthy of Noticing? Good children's literature!

10

Un-Kumbayah Noticings

Many of my Noticings are "kumbayah," meaning all happy and sweet and gaga. But These Noticings are not kumbayah. Still, they are true Noticings.

Carpe Diem

I was sitting in a café. At the table next to me were two young women, evidently college students since they were talking about their papers and exams. The weather outside was beautiful for a winter day. Clear, windless, crisp and sunny.

But the weather report was frightful. We all heard the reporters warn of a huge storm coming in. We heard about the lines in the suburban supermarkets, where everyone was stocking up on milk and toilet paper.

At the next table, one lovely girl said to the other, "I can't believe we will have a storm. It's just so calm and clear." Her friend agreed, "Not a chance. The day is too pretty. The reports must be wrong."

Ah, youth.

With some age comes the knowledge that the storms of life are usually unexpected. One minute all is well. The next minute, terribly not well at all. Life's storms often dump on you most unexpectedly.

So Carpe Diem—seize the day—is the best philosophy of all. What will you Notice today? I believe in celebrating everything you can, especially the small things. Smile at a beautiful sunrise. Sigh happily at a cup of coffee or tea that warms the cockles of your heart. Pat yourself on the back for your hard work… no need to always wait for its result. Noticing and celebrating small things makes for a happy life, and maybe even fortifies you to withstand the next storm.

Conversation-Starter with Teens

What do they think of this Noticing? Perhaps you can
have a conversation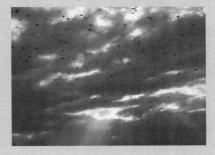
about appreciating the
wonderful things all
around them and about
being happy "in the
moment." A corollary
conversation might be
about the importance of delayed gratification to achieve
a long-term goal. Appreciating things that are "in the
moment" needs to be balanced with understanding that
delayed gratification is often necessary.

Sing in the shower. Dance alone in an elevator. Notice, and
be mindful of the beautiful mix of colors in the sky.

Carpe Diem!

You Never Know

I remember a picture in the newspaper that mesmerized me. Fighters were shooting out of the window of a house in Syria. There were several in uniform, some standing around, some crouched and shooting, one sitting on a sofa while texting. They were in the living room. Furniture looked like it was covered with sheets or blankets. The heavy, ornate draperies were pulled back to allow the fighters to fire their weapons. A huge crystal chandelier hung from the center of the room.

Who had lived there? Surely when they purchased their sofa and easy chairs, their ornate draperies and their elegant chandelier, they never, ever thought the room would be used for war.

When you spend money to decorate your home, you don't imagine soldiers tromping their dirty boots through it. But you never know, do you? You just never know what life may bring. Will you be lucky and live in peaceful times? Will you be caught up in the wars humans fight so often?

I don't know if these fighters were good guys or bad guys—or more realistically—better guys or worse guys. I just know for sure that the woman who selected those drapes and that chandelier was pleased with how elegant they looked, and never, ever thought they would be stained red.

Yes, this is a very un-kumbayah Noticing. But I believe it is essential to Notice these types of things, too. And I also believe

Discuss this un-kumbayah Noticing. In school, students learn about wars, the reason a war was fought, and the strategies used for conducting it. They also learn about numbers of war fighters who were killed. But often, there isn't emphasis on the civilians - how they lived during wars and how their lives were uprooted. This  may be a conversation that your teen would like to have. It can be reassuring to learn how civilians have coped. You might want to discuss "Rosie the Riveter" and some famous Holocaust survivors. Research together online. You may also be able to interview a willing family member or friend who is a veteran.

that when we Notice ugliness in the world, we must be even more mindful to Notice and take time to appreciate its beauty.

Because you just never know.

11

Holiday Noticings

(Back to Happy Stuff)

Thanksgiving

Thanksgiving is one of my favorite holidays because it is cozy, and hopefully, low key. What could be better than a holiday set aside for eating with friends and family, and remembering to be thankful?

Here is some of what I am thankful for: the smell of lemons, the variety of clouds in the sky, the sight of toddlers just learning to walk, Charles Dickens, songs I can belt out loudly and off-key while on the treadmill, summer, laughter, and of course... trash cans.

Ask each family member to keep a log of what they are thankful for throughout the year. They might write in it whenever they have a thankful thought. They can share whenever they want, but make a big deal about sharing the

logs around Thanksgiving each year. Each family member can share as much or as little as they want. Remind them to think about their senses. What do they love that they see, hear, feel, taste, or smell? How about what a specific person has done that they are thankful for?

Merry Christmas!
And Why I Love America

Yesterday, before I went to work, I did some errands up and down the block where I live.

First, I greeted the street vendor and bought a drink from her. "Merry Christmas." she said. She is a Muslim.

Then I went to the market across the street to get some milk. "Merry Christmas," said my friend the check-out clerk. He is a Buddhist.

I was lucky to find the cleaner's delivery truck pulling up as I opened the door to the shop. "Merry Christmas," said the driver from under his Sikh turban.

To each one, I replied with a hearty, "Merry Christmas!" This from a nice Jewish girl.

So Merry Christmas everyone, by which I mean good wishes for peace on Earth, goodwill toward everyone, and hope for a healthy and happy new year. A year in which we all find joy in helping others, our Earth, and the quest for peace.

CONVERSATION-STARTER WITH FAMILY

What kind of diversity do you see in your area? Do people from different countries live near you? Is there diversity in religion, race, ethnic background? Is there diversity of ages? Are there elderly people living near you? Young,

single people? Families? Or is your area mostly homogeneous in some way? How? Who have you talked with, who is most unlike yourself? Was it an interesting conversation?

I Love a Philanthropist
900 Years Old

Since this is a section about holidays, and often people make charitable donations around holidays, I will share this Noticing:

I love the twelfth century Jewish philosopher, Maimonides. Maimonides puts forth eight levels of giving, from the least to the highest:

8. Giving grudgingly.

7. Giving less than one could or should, but willingly.

6. Giving directly to the poor upon being asked.

5. Giving directly to the poor without being asked.

4. Giving when the recipient knows who you are, but you don't know the identity of the recipient.

3. Giving when you know the recipient's identity, but the recipient is unaware who donated.

2. Giving when the donor and recipient are unknown to each other (through a third party).

1. Preventing people from becoming impoverished or lifting them out of poverty by providing a loan, or helping them establish a business, or find employment. This is similar to the ancient Chinese adage: give a man a fish and you feed him for a day; teach a man to fish and you feed him for a lifetime.

Discuss these levels of giving. Each level is good, because to give in any way, is better than not giving. How might each member of the family be a philanthropist in their own way? Can young children contribute  small amounts to a family donation jar? The contents of the jar can be used to donate at the end of a year. Can the family put together a money-raising project and donate the proceeds to a cause?

12

A Silly Amazing Noticing

There is a Clear Winner in This Debate

The debate stage is ready. There are two small tables set a safe distance apart. There is a stool for the moderator. The audience is prepped and quiet. Cell phones are turned off and everyone knows not to shout, boo, or applaud.

An aide appears and lays an object on each table. Mics are tested. The aide walks offstage. The moderator appears, accepts applause, and sits upon the stool. Suddenly, a bright spotlight shines on the two tables.

On the left, a bunch of paper clips lie quietly. On the right, a shiny stapler gleams with pride.

The moderator begins, "Gentlemen, let this be a conversation between the two of you. I will guide the conversation as needed by interjecting clever questions. Let us begin by each of you telling the American people how you can make their lives easier. Paper clips, please begin; you won the coin toss."

"First," said the head paper clip, "let me thank our hosts and my opponent for being here tonight. I am sure, in the course of everyone's preparation, numerous of my brothers and sisters have been clipped to your papers."

"Clipped?!" shouted the stapler. "More like dropped, lost, flung away, stuck together in a useless mess."

"Please, stapler." interjected the moderator. "It's paper clip time. I promise you, you will have your say."

"To answer your question, Madame Moderator, succinctly and without possibility of rebuttal by my misinformed opponent, let me say this: we are small, we are mighty; you can keep us in your drawer or even in your pocket. We are always where you need us." And it did appear that the paperclips were shining ever more brightly on their table.

The stapler began to staple piles of paper that he had set beneath the table. "Staple, staple, staple." he sang as he worked. "What could be more satisfying that the sound of the stapler?! Everything is tied together so securely and neatly! There are no little clips to fall off. When I staple, the job is done!"

The audience burst into applause. "Please!" shouted the moderator. "Audience reaction is not allowed!"

"My job is done cleanly, neatly, and without drawers and cups full of useless little clips." the stapler went on.

The head paper clip could not restrain himself. "If I win this debate, everyone will get free paper clips!" he declared.

The stapler looked at him derisively. "What do you expect people to do with those paper clips?" He looked down his stapler-nose at his opponent. "Do you hope they will open one of them up and pull out a side... so they can clean their nails?!"

The audience erupted again into a huge, "Oooooo! Yuk!"

The stapler stood on his end and looked sincerely at the audience. "Folks," he said, "let's keep our country neat and clean. Let's agree here and now to utilizing the mighty stapler! Discard your paper clips for they are useless, messy, and lead to bad habits."

"Yes!" roared the audience. "Staplers are what we need to move America forward!"

"Our time is up." said the Moderator, forlornly. "I did my job to the best of my ability."

And so the debate ended.

As your Chief Noticing Officer, I must endorse the stapler. Not only is he the best implement to keep papers together; he is also an excellent debater. To be honest, I have always thought the stapler is in the same category as the trash can and the zipper. Long live the stapler!

II.

Annoying Things to Notice

Just a note about Noticing annoying things. My advice is to Notice all you can, but Notice with always a twinkle in your eye and a half-smile on your lips. Cranky with a twinkle is good. Cranky with nastiness, not so much.

1

An Assortment of Cranky Noticings

Cranky—The Un-Kumbayah

I am bothered by the fact that I am not cranky enough.

To remedy this problem, I have spent time thinking about things that annoy me. Here is what is annoying me now:

- "Great Question!" Do journalists really have to compliment each other all the time? They ask each other questions, pre-rehearsed I am sure, and then they almost always respond with "Great question!" As though their colleague is *so* brilliant to ask. I actually like most journalists and I believe their profession is critical, but stop with the "Great question!" already!

- When did it become good form for wait-staff in a restaurant to remove your plate when you are done, but others aren't? I think it is totally rude to leave someone eating by themselves, while everyone else at the table is sitting with nothing but tablecloth in front of them. I was taught not to clear the table until everyone was done. Why did that change? I still think it's very rude. People can sit with their finished plate in front of them until everyone is done!

- Am I the only person in the world who cannot touch saran wrap, press and seal, sealing tape, or anything else that is a sticky tapey-type thing without getting myself all bollixed up? No, I did not do well in kindergarten. Holidays are an extremely dangerous time of year for me, what with packaging up leftovers from holiday meals and wrapping gifts. There must be a simpler thing that can be invented

Conversation-Starter with Family

For a change of pace at dinner, go around the table and have everyone say what annoys them! Remind them that they need to keep the "twinkle in their eye and a half-smile on their lips." No nastiness allowed. This has to be done in good humor, but it can be a good release of tension and hopefully generate some laughs.

to do the trick. Something that doesn't leave me trapped in saran wrap. Let's have a little love for the clumsy and inept!

So there you have some crankiness. More to follow!

Top 10 Annoying Things

1. Always having to have top 10. Or best 5. Or worst 5. Or 12 new ways to cook chicken. Or 3 things you absolutely must know before you step out of your house.

That's it.

My 'Top 10' are really just one hugely annoying thing!

Look at any popular magazine. A title must have a number. Why? Are we so easily beguiled by advertising firms' formulas that we must, absolutely MUST, know the top 10, or 5, or 12? If a title said, "Interesting New Ways to Cook Chicken," or "Simple Guidelines to Follow When Investing," would we not read them?

You may say, "Jeez, she is really easily annoyed!" And, you would be correct.

Imagine a scenario where a most wise and learned person wrote an essay entitled, "Things We Must Do To Save The World." The editor says to him, "Well, even though you didn't number your insights, you have 6. And 6 is such an unwieldy number. 5 sounds so much better. I will edit it to make it 5, and call it "5 Things To Save the World."

And because of this editing…

… the world ends.

It was the 6th idea that was the key.

The crux of this annoyingness is "the sameness." The sameness of all these magazine articles; the predictability, the assumption that of course this is the way it must be.

But, although I am an irascible grouch, I do worry about being out of touch with trends, so I will close this diatribe with:

10 Adjectives That Should Not Characterize Anything

1. Clichéd

2. Trite

3. Overused

4. Hackneyed

5. Dull

6. Worn-out

7. Tired

8. Stale

9. Tedious

10. Mind-numbing

Harumph!

And Another Thing....

I hate passwords!

Everything you want to do requires a password! I can't tell you the number of times I have clicked on something and a page comes up with a login, and I just say @#^%! Who knows what my password is?! And I give up right away because I have no patience and no stick-to-itiveness.

Of course, you're supposed to use different passwords for different things. Otherwise, when hackers hack, your life will be ruined. Surely, someone out there now knows all the shoes I've ever bought! I need to be in a witness protection program or something.

So I have tons of passwords. Who knows which is for what? I read somewhere that you should use the first letters of the first line of books or something... so I have all kinds of nonsense passwords.

Most of my passwords are written in a notebook. Now where is that notebook? Of course, sometimes I don't write them down in the notebook at all because I can't find it.

I am totally ticked off just writing this. Passwords are the enemy! You devils, whom I have written about before, you need to invent something simpler than having us remember a gazillion passwords!

Iwtbot87

Ha! Guess where that password comes from!

CONVERSATION-STARTER WITH FAMILY

Come up with different ideas for passwords, like the first letters of the first line of a book. The trick, of course, is that you have to be able to remember the password.

Come ON! Really?!

I know, I know. I am totally out-of-it. But the only TV I watch is the news. And the commercials that interrupt the news. And I am so very, very annoyed.

I've complained before about how every disease, real or exaggerated, gets an acronym on TV and a drug to control it. These are listed with only minor side effects that may, though not too very often, cause death. (Just because I pee a lot, doesn't mean I have a disease that needs a drug! Mr. Crapper perfected the toilet to solve that problem. But I digress.)

Anyway, most commercials are drug commercials. When not warning you in quiet tones that they could cause you death, and, albeit infrequently, the growth of a second head; they show you the great benefits if you just pop a pill. There is something that may be of interest to some men, but the benefits they display involve sitting in a bathtub next to your partner... who is in a second bathtub. It's odd. I don't know anybody who has two, old-fashioned claw-foot bathtubs sitting side by side.

Please don't misunderstand. I know there are many drugs that are miracle-workers. They treat serious disorders and are wonderful discoveries. However, I think the advertisements go way overboard to convince us we need drugs for everything.

My prime example today is a remedy I saw advertised, that suggests you simply pop a pill any time you feel the pressure of daily living! All day long! They say, the pressures of work, commuting, and

Conversation-Starter with Teen Girls

Discuss how appearance changes with normal aging—wrinkles, grey hair, etc. Is it important to look "forever young?" Why or why not? How do advertising images play into what we think is optimum appearance? Are drug companies doing people a service by developing drugs to reduce wrinkles and other indications of normal aging, or are they just looking  for ways to convince people that they need these things in order to make more money?

Conversation-Starter for Your Group of Women Friends

How do we really feel about the appearance of aging? Are we happy that the drug companies develop drugs for enhancing appearance, or do we think their advertising is doing harm? Why or why not? Why is there an emphasis in the US on a youthful appearance? Is this true in other countries? How do powerful women in our country enhance their appearance? How about powerful women in other countries?

children can all cause stress, so just reach for xxx to help you manage. They even have a version for children! *Children!* I find that absolutely unconscionable.

Noticers, promise me that when you feel common stress, you will use your brain and figure out how to deal with it, instead of making some drug manufacturer rich.

But let us move to another example, before I decide to pop that pill to fix the stress that the pill commercial caused me.

If you are like me and out-of-it, you think an apple is something to eat. Or you hope you could be the apple of someone's eye. Or you are forever grateful that an apple fell on Newton's head, and therefore, we are all stuck on Earth instead of flying off every which way into space. Or you might think of a computer.

Wrong! Not according to the commercials. According to the commercials, we have apples in our cheeks which... *horror*...will fall as we age! How many times have you looked around to see whose cheek apples are falling? "Jeez! Look at those low cheek apples!" you say. But don't worry, there is a drug to inject in your cheeks which will raise them apples right back up!

Whew! How do you spell relief? (Oh. That's another commercial.)

These drugs, you probably know, can be injected different places to solve the problems of aging. No, I don't mean truly serious diseases or the more common afflictions like heart disease, arthritis, or eye problems. I mean "parentheses." Yes! Those terrible little lines at the edges of our mouths. They must be eliminated! Nobody should have "parentheses," as they are called by the doctors with the needles.

But I am about to put all those docs out of business. I have a secret to tell you. You don't need drugs. The way to rid yourself of "parentheses" is—*Dada dada*! (Trumpets blowing off-stage)

SMILE!

Go ahead. Try it.

See. You are beautiful! And you—oh, you are most handsome!

Haha. Take that, Big Pharma! We Noticers will keep you in line with a smile.

Believe Me –
The Emperor Really Is Naked!

Remember the Hans Christian Andersen fable, *The Emperor's New Clothes*? A swindler convinced the Emperor that he had made him the finest costume of all, when in fact, he only made an imaginary garment, and happily pocketed the huge sum paid for it.

This kind of thing happens a lot. Maybe you have examples?

In yesterday's newspaper, I found concrete evidence that 'The Emperor's New Clothes' are being designed all the time.

This time, it's about what gourmet chefs are trying to convince us are the finest of all concoctions... fish spines, lamb hearts, egg shells, pineapple skins!

They're cooked and cooked until they're finally digestible. They're wrapped in sauces until they're finally palatable. They're given poetic names so that they're barely pronounceable. And then they're given enormous prices, so that they become valuable!

If you buy a fish "collar" for two dollars, and sell it as a dish for forty, you're doing well as a business.

But as a consumer, I actually don't want to pay top price for bones, offal (there's a reason it's called that), shells, and skins! Yuk!

People, believe me: The Emperor is naked!

Conversation-Starter with Family

Discuss rip-offs. For example, what does the fashion industry try to sell for high price that is really silly? How about high fashion on the runway? Are there any current fads that look terrible on everyone? Are really expensive sneakers worth the money? What other types of things  do you think are overpriced? Discuss why people pay for things that are obviously not worth the price. Discuss the power of advertising. Do the kids think they're influenced by advertising? How?

Maybe I Should Take Them Up on It and Pole Dance

I have a very grouchy gripe. In fact, it is a great, grouchy, grousing, growling gripe about a grueling gambit.

I wonder if they reproduce sexually or asexually like bacteria. I would guess the latter... like dangerous brain-eating bacteria.

I am talking about "great deals."

Once, in a moment of millennial generation envy, I bought a coupon for a half-priced meal at a local restaurant. Everything went well; I ate there and used my coupon. But never, in my wildest dreams, could I have imagined what would happen next.

My "great deal" emails went from one a day, to two a day. From one company's deals, to three company's deals. To deals from ten companies every hour, to deals stuffing my inbox every minute of every day! I was invited to pole dance, to drink margaritas 'til the cows came home, to take a quick excursion to who-knows-where.

If I saved all the money they offered in these deals by buying their coupons, I would surely end my days in debtors' prison. Their gambit was to get me to spend money I had no intention of spending. My gambit was to delete before I read. I should unsubscribe to all these companies, but that would be a full day's work.

Can someone tell me about an organic, environmentally friendly pesticide that will get rid of asexually multiplying deals?

CONVERSATION-STARTER WITH FAMILY

Talk about the concept of saving money by watching for bargains. When does this make sense? What could be a pitfall? What would happen if your family bought everything it saw that was on sale? How can you balance saving money through bargain hunting, with saving money by not spending at all?

Words are Beautiful!

Why can't we use them?! I don't like acronyms!

Things seem to be getting worse and worse in this department. You'll see on TV that you can't have a descriptive disease anymore. Instead, you must have something that is described by three frightening letters. I have AAI* syndrome. There is no help.

Would you believe... my kitchen trash can is proudly marked in big letters: FPR!

FPR? What the heck is that? A warning: Fear Produce in my Refrigerator? A call to political action: Face Proudly the Reactionaries?

No. It means Finger Print Resistant. Well, there's a vital product. I spend a lot of time putting my hands all over the lid of my trash can, and now I can proudly proclaim myself FPR!**

*Annoyance At Idiocy

** Frequently Peckish and Ridiculing

Conversation-Starter with Family

How many acronyms can each family member think of? What does everyone think of the use of acronyms? Are they good timesavers or do they make people lazier? Has anyone ever been in a different environment where they had no clue what people 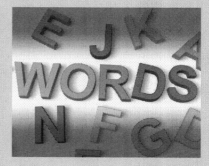 were talking about because they used acronyms?

TV Debate Hell

Do you know what's wrong with this country? TV debates, that's what. The talking head round tables are dragging us down into hell, and the ones that shout at us, have been down there a long time already.

Why, oh *why* must we always have two people debating an issue?! It's so boring!

One side—the other side. It feeds into our pernicious predilection for black/white scenarios: this or that. Yes or no, right or wrong.

I want to see a show called **Shades of Gray,*** because that's the truth much of the time! Or call it **Yes, but ...** or call it **No ... but sometimes**.

Let's rise above the lowest possible denominator for discussion, and actually discuss issues with all the messiness that any issue has around it.

I recently had an eye problem and began to fully appreciate the benefits of seeing clearly. Seeing everything clearly, when you are trying to see who is waving to you down the street, is a blessing. But seeing everything "clearly" when you are discussing issues, is not always a blessing.

Sometimes, a little blurriness makes you more open to the clarity/ blurriness continuum of another person's vision. And that could be very good.

*nothing, absolutely nothing, to do with the best seller

CONVERSATION-STARTER WITH FAMILY

Discuss any issue that's in the news, sports, or even something at school.

Ask each person to give their opinion on the issue. Then ask them what some other reasonable opinions might be. For example, there has been a debate about starting times for high schools. Should the start time be later so that teens can sleep later? If someone thinks yes, then they need to also discuss the opposite view. For example: what will happen to after school activities and sports? What about teens who need to hold jobs after school?

The Gym for Zoftigs

Where is the gym for people who actually need a gym?

I am going to start a gym called: **A Little Zoftig is Not The End of the World**. Zoftig is a Yiddish word that means "maybe I ate dessert one or two times too many, so kill me."

Where I live, gyms are places where people with perfect bodies show them off. What I want is a gym where grandma's arms and a bit of man paunch (maybe more than a bit) are not sneered at. I'm talking about a gym where flabby thighs are de rigueur, and six-pack abs are part of the inner self, not the outer.

We of the Zoftig race want respect and acceptance. Dress at the Zoftig Gym is loose and comfortable, and shows off nothing.

Let me know if you want a membership. We could hang out at the gym a while and then go get coffee... and maybe a Danish?

Conversation-Starter with Teens

Is this Noticing essay amusing? Should we be joking about weight, or should we take it much more seriously? Do your teens see people exercising to show off, to keep in shape, or both? Do they know people who don't exercise because they are embarrassed by the way they look? Should people be embarrassed? Could that be an incentive to exercise and eat healthier, or could it cause them to just give up?

Kill the Clichés

At the end of the day, we should all think out of the box. If fact, don't just think out of it, leap out of it… to your untimely demise.

I am really cranky today! Let's look at this *through the lens* of crankiness.

Why do we all have to spout the same clichés and think we are original? I simply *cannot get my head around that.* Let's *get granular* and figure it out.

Did you *drink the Kool-Aid* on this one? *The ball is in your court.* What clichés drive you crazy?

CONVERSATION-STARTER WITH TEENS

Talk about all the clichés everyone can come up with. Do they think clichés are necessarily bad things? Are they a mark of lazy thinking, or are they a good shorthand that helps everyone understand the point being made?

2

Totally DeTestable
Technology™

This series of Noticings is about technology that is unnecessary, and often doesn't even work. Besides, it is usually too complicated for an impatient grump like me to figure out!

Totally DeTestable Technology™

Yo! Inventors and engineers! Why do you design things that are not only unnecessary, but leave us worse-off than before you came along with your brilliant invention? I'm getting steamed just thinking about this.

For example... *self-flushing toilets*! Guess what, you engineers and architects: Most of these toilets don't flush! First you have to go from stall to stall looking for a flushed toilet. Then, if you're lucky enough to find one, you go in, do your thing, and try your best to figure out how the goldarned thing will flush.

You wave your hand over anything that looks like it could be a laser; you dance around the toilet trying to get something to happen; but no luck. The only thing you can do now, is open the door and leave, hoping nobody is waiting. If someone is, you have to let them know that the toilet is malfunctioning.

As you try to get the water to turn on in the no-touch faucet (another story), you hear the blankety-blank toilet flush behind you. What's that all about? We can push down a handle! It's not too hard!

And while we're on the subject; why can't we have a key for our cars? We still have to keep the key fob in our pocket or purse, so it's not like we've solved the problem of lost keys or anything. Did you think it was too hard to turn a key in an ignition? This stupid invention makes it very difficult to be sure the car is actually turned off properly.

Kids and teens love technology and seem to get it. And men will never admit they don't know how to use something. So, ladies, what say we get together over a glass of wine and yell about all this stuff  until we are bent over with laughter?

Ultra quiet cars are another stupid invention. They're very dangerous for pedestrians. I understand car manufacturers are considering putting fake noise in the cars to cover up the quiet. This is all very strange engineering! For goodness sakes, turn a key, hear a roar, drive! Them was the good old days.

Finally, I must inveigh against "ultra" detergent. The containers can be just as big and heavy as the old ones, but you're not supposed to use as much in each load. So what do they have? Measuring lines inside the caps that are impossible to see! Am I the only one who shines a flashlight into the cap to see where the detergent is? People: make the measuring line in black! Whoa, I am brilliant! I must patent that black line.

Well, yes, I am crotchety today.

More Totally DeTestable Technology™

I told you so!

Did you see the news reports about the bacteria lodging in automatic faucets? So these sinks are dirtier than the ones that you simply turn a handle to work. Apparently the bacteria lodge in the extra bits and pieces needed to make the faucets automatic.

But of course, we all know they're not automatic at all. They're stubborn, and only work when they feel like it, which is often never. And now we know that they're too darn lazy lying in their own multiplying filth to even consider doing their job of cleaning others.

Hospitals are getting rid of them! *Haha*! Take that, you despicable examples of Totally DeTestable Technology!™

Conversation-Starter with Family

When the family is gathered for dinner, without warning, begin to pantomime trying to get an automatic faucet to work. Have the family guess what you are doing. Laugh! Have they had the experience of automatic faucets that don't work? Can they think of other examples of Totally DeTestable Technology™?

Totally DeTestable Technology™... *or Totally Something Else?*

"OMG! You are single-handedly going to bring down the whole industry! Already, with your questions, you have made this iPhone so unhip, nobody can use it anymore!"

Yes, I finally had to give up my BlackBerry, which I routinely slept with, since it became as old and decrepit as my knees, and like them, refused to bend. The BlackBerry roller bar is akin to a knee. If it don't move, don't nothin' move.

But I ask you, is that any way for the Chief Operations Noticer (CON) to speak to the Chief Noticing Officer (CNO)? There would be strife in the offices of The Did Ya Notice? Project™, save for this one fact: I know she is right.

Correspondence nowadays suffers because it isn't done on parchment with quill. However, even I succumbed long ago to the siren call of the smartphone. And now, years after everyone else, I finally have an iPhone.

The problem is... that this new smartphone is smarter than I am.

The CON has answered many of my questions about the iPhone, albeit not patiently. However, she refuses to tell me why it sometimes displays long and narrow, and other times, wide and short. I can't figure out how to change it.

I swipe my finger and strange things happen, but they're not what I

Do your teens think parents are generally less technologically astute than they are? If they think so, ask them why. Why do older people sometimes have more trouble learning new technologies? What should they do to become  more adept? Or should they just forget about it altogether and live as Neanderthals?

want to happen. I've stood on my head and done cartwheels, and it still won't move.

Now I know that this iPhone and I do have something in common—we are both incredibly stubborn. But I will win this fight. Someday soon, I will be able to move my phone from the category of Totally DeTestable Technology™ to a new category: Totally Tamed Titan.

Ha! Who knows what I will tame next! I believe I will try my magic on the automatic faucets that turn on by themselves— or don't!

More Totally DeTestable Technology™ Coming!

Hmmm. It seems that engineers are working on the development of cars that won't need to rely on humans for their navigation. They seem to believe that humans are easily distracted, slow-witted, heavy-footed creatures that should not be trusted with a ton or two of fast-moving steel.

They may be correct.

It stands to reason that well over ninety percent of accidents are due to human error. (You might want to peruse my Noticing "Road Rager vs. Granny.") But you can imagine, since I coined the term, Totally DeTestable Technology™, that I would not be in favor of cars being equipped with such smart technology.

At first it sounds logical—this is a good thing! That is… until the car starts malfunctioning and goes flying off at ninety miles an hour to the nearest beach. Now how would that be different from your typical eighteen-year-old male?

And cars do malfunction. It's the very reason why owners of car dealers and repair shops are among the wealthiest one percent.

But I suppose, upon reflection, that I could be persuaded that this is a good idea…… if instead of the benign GPS voice saying, "Please make your next legal U-turn," it yells, "!@#$%! Idiot cut us off! What the @#$% is wrong with you, you @#$%^&! Now I

What do they think of this technology being developed—to have the cars, themselves, take the lead in driving? Cars are being equipped with more and more technology. Discuss the pros and cons of all the new technology—integration with smart phones for

calling and texting, GPS, entertainment, etc. Everything that might seem so cool at first mention has its downside. Discuss how a specific technology might be helpful or harmful. Maybe it's only helpful if used a certain way? Technology is another area where there are shades of gray, so here's an opportunity for discussion.

missed my turn and have to @#$% turn around!"

Ha! I feel better just typing that! Bring on the technology. Add the @#%^. Then we will see if it's DeTestable or not!

III.

Human Idiosyn-Crazies™ to Notice

Human Idiosyn-Crazies™ are those things we all do that are **endearingly dumb**. We should really laugh at ourselves over these. It's important to laugh because *laughing at ourselves provides us the fuel to be kinder to other people.*

We all have Human Idiosyn-Crazies™. Let's give each other a break sometimes. We can laugh *with* our friends and colleagues, rather than laugh at them.

And when you notice Human Idiosyn-Crazies™ in yourself at work or at home, what do you do? Well, *Notice* them. Be ready with a laugh—heck we're all just human. But you do have choices.

You can *deal with* the Human Idiosyn-Crazy™ or *ignore it*, or *just laugh* it off.

Be quickest to laugh, though—and build up your fuel for kindness!

I Spit a Lot

I spit a lot.

Well, let me clarify. I don't spit like a man walking his dog in the woods with a huge *chau* and a loud and prolific *pau*. Ugh, I am getting woozy just at the thought.

No, I do a very feminine *poo, poo, poo* over my right shoulder. Nothing wet. Just pretend.

Uh huh. You guessed it. I am superstitious.

Just at the thought of bringing on the evil spirits, I do my *poo, poo, poo* routine. I'll show those evil spirits who's in charge!

Yep. Salt spilled = salt tossed over right shoulder.

No walking under ladders. So very careful not to break a mirror. And the umbrella is never opened inside.

Knock on wood certainly can't hurt, and maybe it's the key...

Are you a bit crazy like me?

Well, for this Noticing, I did more research than my usual perusal of Wikipedia. This time, I went to WedMD. It said what we all know—when engaging in superstitious behavior, we are trying to exert some modicum of control over the world... foolish people that we are.

Superstitious behavior might even be healthy, since believing good

things will happen—or at least nothing bad—can contribute to positive results. It's like the placebo effect. The placebo effect happens when if you *believe* you are taking a medicine that will work. Often times, the person will end up getting better, even if what they took was just a sugar pill.

Another interesting thing, is that superstitious behavior has no correlation to intelligence. Intelligent people are just as superstitious as anyone else. So now I feel better.

You may run into me crossing the street to avoid a black cat, or studying the grass in search of four-leaf clovers, or carefully avoiding stepping on the cracks in the sidewalk. Picture in your mind a woman watching carefully for the evil black cat or sidewalk crack. She suddenly darts across a street or leaps across the sidewalk. Knock wood she doesn't trip and fall. Do keep in mind the lack of correlation between intelligence and superstitious behavior.

But be forewarned: never stand behind my right shoulder. You may be the recipient of *poo, poo, poo.*

Are you like me? Can never be too careful? Why test the fates? If I weren't a woman, I would surely have a beard right now, after seeing what it did for the Boston Red Sox.

So, whether you face the world with wild abandon, or you are certain to have a rabbit's foot in your pocket, I wish you well. Break a leg!

What Kind of Person Am I?

What kind of person can walk down the street on a cold winter's day, sipping a cup of coffee? People who do this, and I see them every day, look so content, as if the warm liquid turns their innards into armor against the wind.

I want to be a walking-in-the-cold-drinking-coffee type of person.

I buy a cup and the trouble begins. I have three bags to carry and I know I need my gloves. I put the bags down and put on the gloves, pick up the bags again with my right hand and go for the coffee with my left. (Uh oh. Please don't turn this into a story about the difficulties lefties have navigating the world.)

Well, it's impossible to pick up a cup of coffee with a glove on. Put the coffee down. Take the glove off. Try again and finally make it out of the store. I don't look back to see how long the line has grown behind me as I did my glove, bags, coffee routine. Already I am embarrassed.

Soldiering on, I begin to feel like a coffee person in the cold. I take a sip. Ah. Oh! Hot!! OK, does everyone on the street have a burnt tongue?

Marching along, I notice the cup cover getting covered in coffee. I slurp it off but now I see a coffee stain on my jacket. Do I bounce too much? I didn't know I was a walker-bouncer. I try to walk more smoothly, gliding, gliding along. Hmmm. People are looking at me a little too long, as they pass.

Well, I slurp. I sip. Aiii! I drop a bag. Now my hand is wet with coffee. I lick it off, pick up the bags, and move on looking like a

What other things do people do that look so simple....until you try them yourself? Talk about the different kinds of talents people have—some are athletes, some are writers, some are artists, some are musicians, etc. What is each family member good at? This conversation can be about simple things—like keeping school stuff neat or being helpful in the grocery store. Can some family members tell stories about themselves that

are funny—like this coffee slurping story? Remember it is important to laugh at our own Human Idiosyn-Crazies™!

coffee person again...I think.

But it is cold and now my wet hand is red, and what's this?? My nose is running! I don't see other people with chapped hands and runny noses! I see people sipping their coffee like adults!

I start to laugh—bags flapping, hands frozen, nose running, coffee slopping around, and now...tears of laughter running out of my eyes.

Are there two kinds of people in the world? Content coffee drinkers of the street, and...me? What kind of person am I??

Gold and Blue

As a lover of summer, I dread the chill breeze of autumn. But Mother Nature is wise.

Think of babies. Babies scream and kick and tense up, refusing to be comforted. But once they finally relent, their beautiful big faces and wide eyes make you fall in love with them over and over again. Mother Nature was wise to put such adorable heads on those sometimes incredibly loud screamers.

Likewise, Mother Nature paints the colors of autumn to comfort those of us who are summer-lovers. The turning of the leaves makes you catch your breath at its beauty. I am most partial to golden leaves against a sky that is a special autumn blue. Blue and gold.

I always thank Mother Nature for those few precious days when glorious gold brushes the brilliant blue sky... but I am also cursed at this time.

Cursed, yes. Since my life has been punctuated by blue and gold, gold and blue... I have been cursed with ridiculous songs jamming my brain. Camp songs!

My summer camp colors were blue and gold. Color war! Those of you who have been touched by the anachronism of summer camp color war will understand.

To further the degradation of nature's supreme beauty by silly songs, I am sorry to confess that my elementary school's colors

Who has had a song stuck in their head? What song? How did they get it to stop? What should be done about this Human Idiosyn-Crazy?™ Should it be laughed off? Maybe, unless it's driving you crazy. Should it be ignored? Maybe, unless

you're singing it out loud and driving everyone else crazy. Should it be dealt with? But how? How do you get rid of the song in your head? You can Google this problem and see what solutions come up. Here's one: http://science.howstuffworks. com/life/songs-stuck-in-head1.htm

were also blue and gold. Camp songs and elementary school songs sullying the beauty of the season...

"Blue and gold, blue and gold, blue and gold, blue and gold. Colors that never do grow old. To us you have been royal, and to you we'll always be loyal, our dear old, dear old, Whittier School."

Why? Why, oh why? Why can't I enjoy the soaring autumnal amazement without my brain dipping down into the gutter to retrieve songs from camp and elementary school?!

Robert Frost begins his treasured autumn poem, "Two roads diverged in a yellow wood." Why can't my brain recite that beautiful poem as I gasp at the golden autumn trees, rather than this:

> *The Blues are coming and we won't give in*
> *Our team is fighting 'cause we're gonna win!*

or

> *Gold is our strength and gold is our spirit*
> *Gold is our power. Get on your feet and let's hear it!*

Another Strange Phenomenon

My home office is a very small room. There is no space to be wasted. My desk is pretty much taken up with my laptop and the humongous screen I need so that I have some chance of seeing what I am writing. There is little room for scribbling notes on paper—which I do all the time, even though I can rarely read my handwriting. But somehow, I find space on the desk to store various containers filled with stuff. What stuff? Well let's see…

Binder clips, paper clips, staple remover, pages of explanations about a medicine that I took a few years ago, business cards of people I don't know, stamps (are stamps still 32 cents?), several keys to who knows what, flash drives with who knows what on them and I don't have time to go through them all to find out, a pedometer, a load of buttons—none matching, campaign buttons, and fortunes. "You are on the verge of something big." Yea! Hopefully "verge," will mean very, very soon! (Although… I am sure that I have had this fortune for years…)

I bet you have these types of treasures in your possession too, don't you?

But these containers full of stuff are not what I'm concerned about. What I'm concerned about are the five mugs filled with… PENS!

Pens! What's going on with pens? I only use one kind of pen, because I am a lefty and need a specific pen with ink that doesn't smear. You know the lefty writing position—my hand always rubs over what I just wrote.

Conversation-Starter with Family

Does the family have a junk drawer? Most families do, and it is often in the kitchen. Have each person in the family write down what they think is in the drawer, and see who gets the most correct. This should be good for a dessert course laugh.

Each person can name things on their own desks that pile up, too. Have each family member bring to the dinner table the most useless thing they keep, and maybe something that they didn't even realize they had until now!

Anyway, I understand why I have many of those pens. (Bic Grip Roller Fine Point—in case you suffer lefty-ness too.) But where did the other pens come from? And why do I have four other mugs filled with them (as well as the occasional emery board)? I have no idea if they even work, since I don't use them.

Well, why don't I throw them away? They're wasting precious desk space. *Well, why don't I?*

Do you suffer from this affliction too?

I can't seem to part from these pens. I am worried though. If they're like the chatchkes in the closet that I write about, and

I think they are, then they engage in hanky-panky as well. And the next time I look there will be six mugs of pens, then seven, then eight then...!

This is reminding me of The Sorcerer's Apprentice and the multiplying brooms... *Help!*

What do you do with licentious pens that have a mind of their own?

Mistakes and Excuses

I am an uneducated ignoramus. Well, I probably shouldn't be that hard on myself. After all:

- I am a busy person and can't be expected to know every little detail of every little thing. (The Huffy and Puffy Excuse)

- People love to find fault and nitpick. This tiny mistake is hardly worthy of note. (The Denigrating Excuse)

- The vast store of poetry that I know should be noted, not unimportant details about the poet. (Rationalization Excuse)

- At least I didn't misquote the poetry, which others often do. (Another Denigrating Excuse)

- Oh, shut up! (Regressive Excuse)

What in the world am I going on about? Well, I made a mistake in one of the blast emails I send out about my Noticings, and it made me think about how we humans respond to our own mistakes.

If we think we're knowledgeable, but it's pointed out that we're incorrect, we are likely to make excuses rather than just say, "Yes, I made a mistake." We often say things similar to the excuses listed above.

As always, I did my ten minutes of research. I found a lot written about cognitive dissonance. Often, we react badly to learning of our own mistakes, due to the phenomenon of cognitive dissonance.

Conversation-Starter with Family

Does everyone agree that it's difficult to admit mistakes? Discuss why. Are the kids afraid of being punished? Are they afraid that others will make fun of them? What are some other reasons? Discuss why it's important to admit mistakes. Do they like people  better when they admit mistakes or when they refuse to admit them? How do they feel (or how would they feel) when a parent admits a mistake? What does everyone think of politicians who usually say "mistakes were made" instead of "I made a mistake?" This Human Idiosyn-Crazy™ of having trouble admitting to mistakes needs to be dealt with, don't you think?

Be a Hero at Work Conversation-Starter

People who admit their mistakes and offer to correct them are actually very powerful people. When you are confident enough to admit your mistakes, other people trust and even admire you. Try it—lead by example.

This is when we're confronted with information that conflicts with what we already "know." It knocks us off balance, and then we have to figure out how to regain our stability.

But let me try to be more "emotionally evolved" than my first huffy and puffy excuse would indicate. I will try to heed Ben

Franklin who said, "He that is good for making excuses is seldom good for anything else."

Here's the deal, in my blast email, I quoted Joyce Kilmer and his poem, "I think that I shall never see, a poem lovely as a tree." I referred to Joyce Kilmer as a "her," but Alfred Joyce Kilmer was a married man with five children. Although, he was admittedly in touch with his feminine side when he admired his tree - he didn't feel the need to create a simile about a tree branch as a sword; instead he talks of snow in the tree's bosom.

Whoa, whoa, whoa! Now what's with that last paragraph I just wrote?! A little huffy and puffy soliloquy to show off? A little rationalization to show why one might think he was a she?

OK. OK. In the name of Ben Franklin, I confess. I made a mistake. I erred. I am an uneducated ignoramus. And to think… my mother was an English teacher!

Oh—and by the way—tons of people corrected me.

So, I made a mistake. But that means that huge numbers read my emails and Noticings. That means I am a popular writer with a large following! And… a boorish incorrigible who always has to get in the last word, and come out on top.

I think that I shall never see
An excuse better than one that glorifies me!

Say Cheese

I recently had to get my driver's license renewed. My picture alone would be enough to convict me of any crime by a jury of my peers. But I would appeal it, on the grounds that we need to see the driver's license pictures of each of my twelve jury convictors. Then we'll see whose picture is more evil-looking. But I digress.

My point is this: When did we begin to smile for the camera?

The DMV didn't give me enough time to settle my face into an upstanding citizen look, let alone a pleasant smile. And this is most distressing, because what good is a driver's license picture anyway? I always thought it was to soften the heart of the traffic cop when he was deciding whether to ticket me for speeding, or just give me a warning. Obviously, such a law-abiding woman (as testified by her upstanding picture) would not be a speeder; it must have been just a slip of the foot. But I digress.

Have you seen pictures of your relatives several generations back? I have two large photos in the back of my closet. Unfortunately, I don't know who they are, but I do know I wouldn't want to mess with them. They glare at me through the centuries with their stiff demeanors. People just didn't use to smile for the camera.

I did my usual diligent research (I Googled) to determine why, and to find out when smiling actually began. Here are a number of reasons why people didn't smile for the camera:

- There were very long waits for exposures. Who can smile like a dolt for long periods?

Conversation-Starter with Family

Can you find photos of grandparents and family members from even earlier generations? Can the kids find family resemblances in the faces or the expressions? It would be fun for the kids to hear stories that you may know about "the olden days."

And try this, parents: take pictures of each person in funny clothes and/or with the funniest expressions on their faces that they can think of. Let the pictures stay in your camera or phone lest siblings tease each other by showing them at school...

- To "help" people hold still, photographers used head clamps and opiates to sedate them.

- Teeth were generally bad and not to be shown.

- Culturally, it was thought that smiling was an indication of low intelligence. Men were to appear authoritative; women were to appear contemplative. Smiling simply wasn't appropriate.

But sometime in the 20th century, smiling came into vogue. I would bet that advances in technology made photography easier, fun, and much more common-place.

Now we are all to appear pleasant, at least to some degree.

At play, most of us instinctively smile for the camera. Although, for formal photographs, or head shots, we often appear at least somewhat serious. Before a special occasion or a photography session, we think about how we want to look. Only our mirrors know how much we practice different smiles.

But I know what my next research project will be...

Why do we all have to rest our hands on our chins nowadays? It's hardly a natural position, and yet—look at formal shots today. So many have the hands-on-chin! Why? But I digress.

For now my advice is simple: Say Cheese!

Cicero Was Right on the Money!

In ancient Rome, Marcus Tullius Cicero wrote, "If you have a garden and a library, you have everything you need."

I think that is a beautiful thought. I wish I had more time relax in a flower garden with a good book. I've done it, but infrequently.

There is a beautiful flower garden just a half mile walk from my home in the city. It terraces up and back, so that when you reach the top, you are quite far from the city street, surrounded by flowers, shrubbery, and old stone walkways crumbling and overgrown with greenery.

Cicero's thought is just as appealing if you think about curling up inside with a good book next to a vase of beautiful flowers. This is another just delightful gestalt. In fact, I would call this scenario of reading amidst natural beauty, 'Cicero's Gestalt.'

But before I get too lost in this reverie with an insipid smile upon my face, I want to double back to a grumpy, grouchy thought I had.

If you do indeed have just about everything you need in a garden and a library, why do we surround ourselves with junk that we don't need? There are two catalogues in particular that make me mad: Sky Mall and Solutions. What a load of unnecessary garbage! Totally superfluous, needless rubbish that fills up homes and eventually will stuff up closets.

Here's a perfect example! Some plastic contraption that holds your

(CONTINUED...)

Conversation-Starter with Family

Have you acquired things that are unnecessary? Challenge each person to name one thing they have that they don't really need. Caution: This is a laughing exercise... don't make people discard or give away stuff they still want, if you ever want to have more family conversations! Should overbuying be ignored, dealt with, or laughed off?

Another time, think about things that were totally necessary at one point, but are irrelevant today. Teddy bears, pacifiers, blankies, training wheels, preschooler picture books, etc. Talk about how needs change, but remember that what someone feels strongly about at a certain point in time should not be belittled. You can also talk about things that are necessities now, but didn't even exist a relatively short time ago. Smart phones are an example.

Be a Hero at Work Conversation-Starter

Are there processes or procedures that are not really necessary and could be done more simply? Remember to keep in mind the end goal of the process. Could you achieve the same result in another way that would be faster and easier?

cell phone, keys, or a notepad. You can hang it from anywhere. Ha! Just put your stuff down on a table or the car seat! Why do you need a piece of plastic trash hanging around?

Well, on the other hand... now that I'm thinking about it... it might be good to know where everything is, and it would be easier to keep your keys and phone together...

All right. Here's another example. A battery powered light that you can stick anywhere. Ha! If you have a dark closet, you can just use a flashlight! Why do you need something else? A flashlight works fine. I use it myself!

Well, on the other hand... I really could use that light on top of my washing machine... and then I might as well get another for my closet...

OK. OK. Here's another: they sell those mops that are extra long and can clean the tops of bookshelves or ceiling fixtures. Oh boy. Those stupid things are so long that they are impossible to store. You could just get on a ladder with a rag and do the job!

I know about this mop because I actually did buy this once. But it kept falling out of the closet, it was so cumbersome. I threw it out after a year. At least I think I did. I don't know where it is. Maybe it's still in a closet somewhere. But I know one thing for sure. I never did use it. And truth be told, I never did get up on a ladder with a rag either...

Hmmmm. OK, I confess. I just took a break from writing this to find the mop and dust the top of the bookshelves. Wow! That was time well spent!

Ok. So I've been having some trouble so far proving my point that we don't need all this trash they try to sell us... but at last I have found something!

The Box of Applause and The Box of Laughter! Each $24.95. When you lift the lid of the boxes, you hear applause or laughter!

OMG! Please laugh at my Noticings and give me some accolades before I spend fifty bucks on this!

I Am Boring

Now, now. Don't be so quick to agree!

But really, I'm worried about myself. Please tell me you do these things too. Maybe we can start a Boring Club. Very exclusive.

So here's one thing... I eat out a lot, both for business and with friends. I go to a wide variety of restaurants, but if I've been someplace a couple of times....I always order the same thing. The menus are full of interesting choices, but I, as a dull person, barely glance at it.

If I'm in a plain old deli type place, I order roast turkey on rye with mustard. If I'm in a Vietnamese restaurant, I order lemongrass chicken on a bed of noodles. If I'm in an upscale American bistro, I order a salad with grilled salmon. Chinese, it's veggie fried rice. Thai, it's tofu with ginger. Pizza, it's Neapolitan. Dinner at an American place, always the fish. Italian, fish if upscale; penne primavera, if casual. Even Ethiopian can be guessed—vegetarian combination platter. No, I'm not a vegetarian, just boring. I will confess that if I'm someplace that has locally sourced, grass-fed beef, I'll have a hamburger. No cheese, just lettuce, no mayo nor the more melodic aioli. (I said I am boring; I forgot to confess that I am also a food snob.)

How about appetizers? Always the beet salad.

How about dessert? Ah, just gimme the berry tart and be done with it!

And I'm not just boring food-wise. Although I like to look sharp

Conversation-Starter with Family

What boring habits does each family member have? Have each person list their boring habits. Smile! Is anyone up for some change?

Be a Hero at Work Conversation-Starter

Sometimes at work we fall into roles. Are you a person who doesn't speak much at meetings? Are you a person who initiates all the parties? Are you a person who has lunch with other team members, or who never does? Try coming out of your role. Shake things up (in a good way) for yourself. Don't  negatively surprise your teammates, though. If they assume you will organize the party, be sure and recruit someone else before you give it up. Be positive and thoughtful of others, but push yourself out of your comfort zone a bit.

when I am at work, truth be told, I wouldn't object to wearing the same thing every day. In fact, when I get home, I always change into the same jeans and the same type of shirt. (Yes, I wash them sometimes.) I fear that if I didn't go to work, I would always wear the same clothes. And, although I won't describe my outfit, I always sleep bedecked the same.

Well, I'm on the roll now to prove my boringness. Why do I

always brush my teeth before I wash my face? Why not vice versa to shake things up a bit? When I work out, it's always the same things in the same order. Oh yeah, back to food—I always eat the same breakfast, too.

Aiiii! As I look around me for more evidence of my boringness, I see my usual drink sitting beside my computer! A glass filled ¾ with water and ¼ with orange juice.

Of course! That never changes either.

My god, I am bound and determined now to break out of my habits! I am off to buy cranberry juice for my water!

Are you boring too? Break out with me! Instead of the Boring Club, let's buy cranberry juice together!

What's your metaphorical cranberry juice? Please tell me I'm not the only boring person around... *Please!*

Sweet Thievery

Waiting in line at the store for the self-checkout stations, I watched a toddler standing next to his father who was scanning items and dropping them into his bag. The items were boring, one plain old box after another. Next to the father and toddler, was another man checking out more interesting things.

The toddler watched the other man intently. Suddenly, as quick as you can imagine, the toddler hopped to the next station, took the man's ice cream from the scanner, jumped back to his father's bag and dropped it in!

The entire line erupted in laughter. The father looked around, startled, as did the other people at check-out. When the father realized what his son had done, he firmly made him take it out of the bag and return it to the rightful owner, who, to his credit, was also laughing.

The father, as parents are wont to do, ordered his son to apologize. The little thief murmured something and all returned to normal.

But I wonder if the toddler shouldn't get some credit here. He knew what he wanted, and he got it. There's something to be said for setting a goal and making it happen. Maybe the toddler knew it wasn't quite the right thing to do, because he was awfully quick about his business. But there's something to be said, too, about figuring out the obstacles and how to overcome them.

I see the makings of a successful adult here. I just hope the father

Am I right here? Is this the best way to handle the situation? Or should the father be more severe in his disapproval? Should the father have taken the toddler out for ice cream? And is it a good idea to make toddlers apologize?

next took him to an ice cream store, and discussed ethical and moral behavior... over a double scoop cone!

My Way is the Only Way

You know, I am the only one who can properly load a dishwasher.

What's that, you say? YOU are the only one who does that correctly?

I have noticed that there are many misguided souls who believe that only they can load properly. Why are we modern humans so strongly attached to our own methods of dishwasher-loading?

How about folding socks? Are you the only one who does that correctly as well? Well, I just hope you turn the left one over the right, and not vice versa!

Might I enquire as you how you store your cups in the cupboard? Hopefully handles to the left, not to the cursed right! Although my proclivity on this score might devolve from the fact that I am a lefty.

You do know, I trust, that toilet paper unrolls from the over side, not under.

I am certain that you are grateful for my guidance on these critical issues. Of course, there are many other tasks of daily living that require the proper methods. Please weigh in.

Conversation-Starter with Family

If you have a dishwasher, how is it loaded in your house? Have you Noticed how you fold your socks? How about that toilet paper? What other things that you're sure you are doing the "right" way?

Secrets of the Closet

In my Noticing entitled 'Maybe I should Take Them Up On It and Pole Dance,' I discussed the problem of asexually reproducing online deals. Well, I have discovered something else that reproduces asexually.

Or maybe not. Maybe it reproduces the old-fashioned way. Who knows what goes on in the darkness of the closet.

Yes! I am talking about *crap*. I am talking about *stuff*. I am talking about *chatchkes*.

How does it happen that a once pristine closet morphs itself into a clone of Fibber McGee's?*

It obviously happens because Shenanigans happen in that closet. Of this, I am sure! Certainly, a neatnik like me would not be collecting a mess and stuffing it into a closet.

Fourteen years ago I moved into my home. Prior to that, I lived in a home for twenty years. I had cleaned out everything before the move. Thrown out. Sold. Donated.

I began life in the new home with plenty of closet space. What a luxurious existence, opening my closet doors and grinning at the sight of neatly arranged articles surrounded by open space.

Ahhh—but wicked things soon ensued.

What have I encountered lately in my closets? Six thousand thermos bottles. Two bookends; that is two different bookends

Do they think this Noticing is funny? Maybe mildly so? C'mon, make me feel good! Do they think the same thing is happening in their closets?

Should this "chatchkes in the closet" problem be ignored, laughed off, or dealt with? I say you should deal with *your* messy closets, but *mine* are just fine as is…

without mates. Nine ice cube trays, and I never make ice cubes. Seven glass vases from florist deliveries. A very odd shaped vase or candle holder or something. Eighty-two hundred different cables and cords. Eight old cell phones and one clunky old telephone/answering machine. More untouched exercise balls, yoga materials, exercise CDs, videos, and tapes than I can count. A ceramic frog. Two broken fax machines. A showroom full of humidifiers and vaporizers. And on and on…

Where did all this come from? I certainly didn't buy it all. I don't remember receiving gifts of vaporizers or ice cube trays. The only answer is… Shenanigans.

Unprotected shenanigans in the darkness of the closet. And I am left to deal with the progeny!

I only hope the chatchkes enjoyed themselves.

*Fibber McGee was the star of a TV show from the 1950s. He was famous for his closet. He would open the door, and since it was stuffed so full, everything would fall on his head. Well, it was funny back then...

Ketchup on the Side, Please

I was grabbing some orange juice from my refrigerator, when it struck me.

On my refrigerator door, as on the doors of millions of American refrigerators, stood a bottle of ketchup, a bottle of mustard, a bottle of mayonnaise, and bottles of various other concoctions.

As I gazed on these bottles, a most critical question came to my mind.

Why will I eat a turkey sandwich only with mustard, while I will eat a chicken sandwich only with ketchup?

I realize that many other people reverse these rules and eat ketchup and mustard in all kinds of unruly ways. To me, a hamburger must have ketchup, never mustard. A hotdog must have mustard, never ketchup. Relish is fine for both. But mayonnaise, oh mayonnaise! This may only be eaten mixed with tuna fish… never with meat!

Now don't fight me on this. I know you drown your meat sandwiches in mayonnaise. I will not deign to comment on that.

Why do we have such set ways to eat? Go to any diner and listen to the patrons order. Heaven help the wait staff if the condiments are not correct.

This is a Noticing about old-fashioned American eating. Let it be known that I believe a meal can be greatly enhanced by salsa or chutney. And guacamole. Bring it on! The more, the better!

Conversation-Starter with Family

Think about ketchup, mustard, relish, mayo, salsa, guacamole, hot sauce, chutney and any other condiments you can come up with. Go around the table and have everyone say one thing they will eat only with ketchup, then go on to mustard, then relish, etc. Hopefully you'll all disagree and be laughing your heads off. This is another  Human Idiosyn-Crazy™ that we can laugh at ourselves about.

Here's a cautionary tale, if you have a tendency to become gluttonous like me. I was at a lovely reception with a huge buffet table. As I moved around the table filling my plate, I spotted a large bowl of the aforementioned cherished guacamole. I piled it on, hoping nobody was watching.

As I moved away from the table, I put a huge forkful of the lovely green spread in my mouth. I knew I should be more ladylike in my eating, but I am crazy about guacamole.

My eyes opened wide and tears streamed down my cheeks. I looked for a way to empty my mouth without being hugely gross. I ran to the bar for water. People made way for me as I leaped to the front of the line and gulped down the proffered water from a bemused bartender.

I had stuffed a huge amount of wasabi into my mouth.

Some people, I guess, should just stick to basics. Ketchup and plain old yellow mustard, used in their proper places, of course.

Coming Out of The Magoo Closet

Yes, that was me. Sitting at a board room table at a very important meeting, refusing to get up for any reason whatsoever.

People looked at me strangely since I usually get up and greet people when they arrive and when they leave. But not this time. This time I would not budge.

Nor would I back my chair up and cross my legs comfortably as I listened to the conversation. Not this time. This time I had my chair so close to the table that I could only sit up ramrod straight and stiff.

Furthermore, I hardly looked at the papers in front of me, and hardly took notes at all.

Why was my behavior so stilted and strange?

Well, yours would be too if you showed up to an important meeting wearing a jacket from one suit, and pants from another.

The jacket and pants didn't go together at all—not the color, not the cut. And to top it off, I had selected a bright red shirt so as to draw attention to my authority.

The bright red looked particularly bad with my pants, which turned out to be green.

Now you see why I couldn't stand up. I am, emphatically, not a Christmas tree.

Has anyone ever gone to school or work and discovered they were wearing mismatched clothes or shoes? What did they do? Did they point out their mistake to everyone? Did they try to hide it? Did they pretend that they wore those clothes on purpose? Did they go home as soon as possible and change, or did mom or dad bring other clothes to school? What does everyone think is the best way to deal with a mistake like that?

But what about not reading? Ah, here's where my Magoo-ishness will be confessed. I have worn contact lenses since I was 13 years old. I have particularly terrible eyesight, and only wear my coke-bottle-bottom glasses from the bed to the bathroom in the morning.

Carly Simon's old song, "You're So Vain" was certainly written about me.

Due to an eye problem, I temporarily could not wear those contact lenses. You will agree that a sophisticated, stylish woman (mismatched suit notwithstanding) cannot appear with Magoo glasses. Do you know Magoo? He was a cartoon character long, long ago with particularly terrible eyesight. He didn't wear glasses, so he got into all kinds of trouble.

On a similar note...

There I sat in the meeting, almost sightless, talking solely from memory since there was no way I could read anything. Which, of course, was why I was wearing my maladroit costume. I couldn't really see what I was grabbing from my closet that morning.

So now, I must walk around like this, either almost blind, or Magoo-like, in who knows what odd apparel.

Because of this I have decided that, like the old king of Spain who made the Spaniards all speak with a lisp because he did, and so they do to this day, I henceforth decree that Magoo glasses shall be the latest rage and highest style.

Are you in?

The Ladies Room Lurker

I spend a lot of time in ladies rooms.

This is not a consequence of gastrointestinal issues, but rather a consequence of another affliction altogether. I have a serious and incurable case of hyper-punctuality. I am as busy as anyone, but I cannot countenance tardiness. I am absolutely never late, and have much trouble being on time. I am afflicted with the embarrassment of always being early.

So as not to leave an impression that I don't have enough to do, or worse, that I am not supremely important, I must tarry wherever I can. Usually that means a Ladies Room.

Sometimes, if I am not in the city, I drive in stalling circles around my destination. If I'm lucky, I can pull into a parking lot and actually get some emailing or reading done. I have tried to leave later for meetings, but it just doesn't happen. Because of this affliction of mine, I have little tolerance for meetings that do not start on time or for people who are perpetually late.

Of course, the tardy people may indeed be the flip side of the early people, those like me. If I cannot manage to be "on time," why don't I cut some slack for those who are the reverse of me, but are not "on time" either? Why? Because being early is a virtue recognized by the gods, and being late is simply rude.

As George Bernard Shaw said, "Better never than late."

Of course, Oscar Wilde believed, "Punctuality is the thief of time."

BE A HERO AT WORK CONVERSATION-STARTER

Have a conversation with your team over lunch. Who is always early? Who is always late? Who manages to show up just on time? Who wants to change? Who has ideas to help that person? Are these behaviors a problem? For the person? For the team? This should be a light-hearted conversation. The first person who gets annoyed, gets no dessert. Who is perfect? I see you all raising your hands…

In my opinion, the hyper-punctual people should be left alone. And the late ones...? Beware, oh beware, the wrath of the Chief Noticing Officer.

I really like Oscar, but as I realized today while I spent much time washing my hands in a public restroom, I guess I am doomed to be more like George.

I Am in Great Danger

I am in great danger.

I truly fear that one morning I will not wake.

A killer lurks next to my bed, of this I am certain.

Yet, in some perversity of my personality, I only add to my danger, regularly and recklessly.

I am speaking, of course, of the huge pile of books sitting on my night table. The pile climbs higher and higher towards the ceiling. It is but one bump in the night from tumbling onto my head, and that will be the end of me.

Killed by Dostoevsky. Murdered by Charles Dickens. Put to a very fine end indeed by E.L. James.

Do you keep buying books as well? Books that pile up next to the bed, a sign of great optimism and hope. A sign that the better side of you will actually read these books one day?

All of my books held great interest for me, and some still do. Some are certain to make me a better person. Some are destined to carry me to another, fascinating world. Some will make me laugh and cry. Some will make me fall asleep.

The question is simple: When will I confront this killer? When will I slowly and methodically disassemble, tame, and make him into a being that I can take advantage of? Some may wish to read

in order to empower themselves with knowledge. I wish to read in order to empower myself and finally cut this unstable killer down to size.

Confessions of a Low-Down, No-Good Cheater

I'm sure you're like me. All the things I have to do during any given day, run around in my head like a bunch of mosquitos. Stuff for the family, stuff for work, stuff for friends. Throw in stuff for volunteer commitments and stuff for myself… there is no doubt I'm gonna get bit by one of those mosquitos. I'm sure to forget something.

The remedy for me is to make lists. I love lists! Well, really, I love to cross things off my lists. Crossing an item off a list is like scratching a mosquito bite. Ahhh! It feels so good for a minute or so. But then, the itch comes back… the other tasks are still there to buzz around my head, or to stare me down from the paper.

Sometimes, I have so much going on that I think I'm too busy to make a list. And here is where I turn into a low-down, no-good cheater.

Sometimes… I make a *retroactive* list! There! I said it. I confessed.

Sometimes, after I've done a bunch of stuff, I write it all down on a list, and then take great pleasure in putting a line through each completed task! Ha! Nobody is going to deprive me of the pleasure of my putting the black line emphatically through something!

So I'm a cheater. So what! I have enjoyed the tremendous pleasure crossing things off. Ha! Call me a hedonist, if you will. I will scratch my mosquito bites, and I will cross off my list's items with a vengeance. Either as the rules permit, or *retroactively!*

Conversation-Starter with Family

Who makes lists? Do they enjoy crossing stuff off? Post everybody's list in the kitchen and celebrate all the black lines through stuff! Have a black line party! Have cake! Have ice cream! Then, retroactively, write PARTY on the lists and cross it off... Until next time!

Be a Hero at Work Conversation-Starter

Does your team celebrate enough? Getting through a major part of a project requires celebration! The least you can do is clink your coffee cups together to celebrate the black line you can put through Phase I!

The Texting Pretender

As I approached the corner, I moved to the side of the sidewalk and took my smartphone out of my pocket, so as not to appear as weird as I guess I am.

As I pretended to look at my phone, I closed my eyes behind my sunglasses and savored the heat of the sun radiating on my back.

What do you think about if you have trouble sleeping at night? Do you keep a "sleep aid" in your mind? I always picture myself lying on the sand next to the sea, with the sun beating down on me, warming me from the outside in.

As I stood on the street corner with the sun on my back, I could smell the sea and hear the waves.

But... people were saying *excuse me* as they walked by, and I needed to come back to where I was. Reluctant to return to reality, I walked down the street and kept an eye out for salt water taffy. I knew it was there somewhere, maybe just around the next corner. I could smell it, just as I could smell the sea.

Look kindly on people in sunglasses texting on the summer sidewalk. They may not be the textaholics they appear to be. They may be busy transporting themselves to beaches far, far away.

CONVERSATION-STARTER WITH FAMILY

What is a mental picture each person has, or could imagine, of a happy, calm scene?

This is a Human Idiosyn-Crazy™ that can be very helpful. A good night's sleep is surely of great value.

What I Don't Know

I thought it would be a good idea to catalogue all the things I know nothing about, so I can try to learn something about them. Unfortunately, I will have to live to over two hundred to get to it all, and by then, I will surely be blind, deaf and senile. Oh well, I will start my list now anyway.

I don't know my flowers. This bothers me. I need to learn this. Knowing a daisy from a rose is all I can brag about.

I simply do not understand music. Oh, I like to listen to tunes, but I don't know anything about scales, or musical themes, or whatever most people know. However, I have often been told, that while singing a simple song, I touch on a number of different keys. Is that good?

I don't know about physics. I skipped it in high school. Got out of it somehow and was quite pleased then. Only now, I am still suffering from the folly of a fifteen-year-old's choice.

I think the physics folly contributes to the fact that I don't know about architecture. I know different styles, but I don't know how the building or bridge stays up.

There is so much I don't know about history, I couldn't begin to list the topics.

My gosh, I am beginning to think—*what **do** I know*?

CONVERSATION-STARTER WITH FAMILY

Here's a dinner conversation that mom, dad, or grandparents can dominate. Name things you don't know about. Remind the kids that they have more time to learn about these. If everyone in the family happens to be curious  about a certain topic, you can research it together. By the way, how *do* bridges support the weight of all that traffic?

There is no better Human Idiosyn-Crazy™ than curiosity. It may kill the cat, but it makes us humans rich in knowledge.

The Source of All Knowledge

If you don't already know this, let me make note: I am a sophisticated, wise and witty woman. And well-read, I might add.

Here is my proud confession: I never go to sleep for the night until I have read the comics. I save them for the night since I believe that saving the best for last has its merit, at least when it comes to the comics. I would never read them at breakfast.

The comics are spectacular. They are the source of much of my knowledge. (Aha, you say, now it begins to make sense.) Well, although I also love raindrops on roses and whiskers on kittens, here are a few of my favorite comic things:

Pearls before Swine—I love it! Larry the Croc, Pig, Guard Duck, even Rat. One could not ask for a more stimulating and loveable group of friends!

Judge Parker. Everyone wants to be fabulously rich, fabulously smart, and fabulously kind. If we study this strip enough, maybe we will learn how to do it.

Sherman's Lagoon. Who couldn't love Fillmore?! And Thornton— the polar bear who loves sunbathing on tropical beaches—ah, he has the life! And Sherman's wife, a lovely rotund shark, is so spiffy in her pearls!

Actually, I love almost all the strips. There are two, however, that drive me crazy. One is about an incredibly goody-goody man— ugh! The other includes the most idiotic man you could possibly

CONVERSATION-STARTER WITH FAMILY

Who likes the comics? What are some favorites? What ones are disliked? What ones make no sense at all?

imagine—such a wuss! Can you guess who these guys are? Hints: The first man lives in the woods with his wife, father-in-law, and adopted son. The second lives in a house in the suburbs and likes to play games.

Please tell me I am not the only one with this Human Idiosyn-Crazy™. Does anyone else diligently study the comics?

Thankful for the Weirdness
That Makes Me Happy

You probably know by now that I can be somewhat kumbayah-ish. So, with no apologies, I am going to talk about a few things that make me happy.

You know from 'The Source of All Knowledge' that I'm religious about reading the comics. But here's what makes me especially happy: When I'm finished reading the comics every night, I simply throw them over the edge of the bed onto the floor! Ha! I just toss them overboard! They lie on the floor in a mess. *Tossing them overboard and making a mess makes me happy!* (And yes, of course, I pick them up in the morning.)

Another thing that makes me happy: I use way too much shampoo! I just pile it on and make huge piles of lather on my head. Way too much! Bubbles everywhere! *Haha*! Now you are getting the idea of what a wild and crazy girl I am? *A huge mess of shampoo on my head makes me happy!*

I have ten beautiful, luxurious bath towels with matching hand towels and washcloths. They're large, thick, and fluffy, in beautiful celadon and cream to match my home. They are everything a normal person could want in a bath towel. I never use them. I save them for company. I never use them because I do not like thick, luxurious towels. I have four towels for my own use. They are thin, torn, and raggedy. I wash them every four days because I never use a towel more than once. To the normal person they

OK. Confess. What are the weird things that make each person happy?

We should definitely laugh at ourselves over the Human Idiozyn-Crazies™ that make us happy.

certainly look like cleaning rags. *Using old raggedy, torn-up old towels makes me happy!*

I guess I'm just a comics-tossing, shampoo-wasting, raggedy towel-using, nut. Aren't we all nutty in our own ways? Notice the weird habits that make you happy. Confess! What are they?

Road-Rager vs. Granny

I really am a patient, understanding soul.

But behind the wheel, something happens. I turn into a furious, impatient maniac. Well, not really a maniac. I don't drive crazily, but I do get unreasonably mad at people going too slowly, or too fast, or whatever they're doing to annoy me. I yell and curse (all with my windows up so nobody can hear).

"The gas pedal is the one on the right, Granny!" or "You have a turn signal don't you, Idiot?!"

I researched road rage, and I learned that it's an official mental disorder called "intermittent explosive disorder." Being a jerk is a disorder. I am surprised I have not yet seen commercials for a drug for this… "Do you suffer from IED?"

Anyway, the happy truth is that I am not a jerk, but rather, an unfortunate victim of IED. This means my screaming at other drivers cannot be helped.

But truly, I have really bad eyesight, and driving at night is a challenge. I tend to drive slowly, I sometimes brake when I shouldn't, and there have been times when I've inappropriately used my brights. When people pass me, it really appears that they may be yelling.

There is a very old comic strip character, Pogo, who said, "We have met the enemy and he is us." Well, I may yell at the granny driver by day, but I become the granny driver at night!

Why do a lot of people have much worse tempers when driving than they do the rest of the time? Talk about the dangers of road rage with your teen. It's true that people do things in their car, like curse and scream, that they would not do in public. Discuss why that might be so.

(Hmmm. Neither my road-rager self nor my granny self should be on the road. This Human Idiosyn-Crazy™ needs to be dealt with!)

Who would have guessed that the mirror image of the furious road-rager is the squinting old granny hunched over the steering wheel, inching along? "Get a move on, Granny, or get off the road!" Oops, I mean, "Pass me if you want to, Road-Rager, and let me drive the way I want to."

Wow, I can give myself whiplash just driving day into night…

I Love Big Sunglasses

I love big sunglasses not for fashion's sake, but because my nose is very, very big. Yes, I am extremely nosey and I like to stare. And behind my sunglasses, nobody can tell how rude I am!

As I walk down the city streets, I can really look at people. Humanity is the ultimate motley crew—all shapes and sizes, and all levels of intensity and mood as well. From business-like seriousness to touristy confusion. And the snippets of cell phone conversations… So many relationship issues!

Here comes an older guy in a business suit, must be in his seventies, just walking as fast as his legs will take him. Wow! He needs to get somewhere for important business… or maybe he needs a bathroom.

And here's an interesting looking person… "Oh, honey," I'm thinking, "You don't really want to be walking around in that outfit, do you? Let me get you a mirror."

People are calling their friends to tell them that they can't believe what 'she said to him.' Other people did a great job on a project, but their bosses never appreciate anything.

Now, here is a couple who think they have the next election all figured out.

Hey, what's this? Some lady in big sunglasses is coming over to me. What? She has a big mirror. Oh my! Well, I was in a hurry getting

Is it fun to stare at people and eavesdrop on their conversations? Why? Why is it rude to do that? Do you like people staring at you? Do you think movie and music stars like to be  stared at? What are paparazzi? Why do stars hate them? Or do they?

out of the house and just threw on... Yes, I do know a charity that I can donate clothes to...

Humph! The nerve of some people—so nosey, so judgmental!

What is Wrong with My Brain?!

Please tell me this happens to you too! Please tell me I'm not the only one!

I start out on my commute to work, and of course, I need the traffic report. It's already five after 8:00, and the traffic report is eight minutes after 8:00 (it's always on the "8s"), so I'm pleased I don't have to wait too long. First comes traffic, then comes weather.

I turn on the radio and listen. Someone is talking about the economy, the Middle East, a politician's scandal. Then a commercial, and finally... the traffic report.

But—wait! How can this be? Another commercial?!

The report is already over and I didn't hear a word of it?! Not again, I think to myself... Well at least I will listen for the weather report.

Wait! They're already talking about three days from now! What about today? I missed that too!

Once again, the radio was on, but I didn't hear a thing. No wonder I'm sitting in traffic in the pouring rain with my best shoes on and no umbrella.

What is wrong with my brain? Are you like this too?

CONVERSATION-STARTER WITH FAMILY

Everyone can give an example of a time when they kind of drifted off into their own world and didn't hear a thing. Maybe it was listening to the car radio; maybe it was listening to a teacher; maybe it was listening to a speaker at work. Maybe you didn't Notice what you were  supposed to Notice, but you probably Noticed something else. So all is not lost.

This Human Idiosyn-Crazy™ is the epitome of "endearingly dumb."

Is Tolstoy Right About Families?

"Happy families are all alike; every unhappy family is unhappy in its own way."

This is how Anna Karenina begins. I have been reading Anna Karenina all year, (have you ever taken a full year to read a book? I think I am absolutely disgraceful), and I am still not finished, so I have yet to judge how Tolstoy will prove this to be true.

However, this declaration strikes me as false. Since every family, and every person, is touched by happiness, sadness, worry, sickness, pride, satisfaction, anger and delight. In short—every human emotion. The extent of happiness, is how we make peace with the negatives and are able to focus on the positives.

Some have more trouble making this peace than others, due to illnesses—both mental and physical—and extreme hardship, but nonetheless the extent that one can do that goes far to determine one's level of happiness.

Happy families put up with the foibles of their relatives in a good-natured way. They don't bear grudges, and are helpful to one another. Unhappy families are stuck in a negativity of the past.

So now that I'm thinking out loud, I'm beginning to believe that perhaps Tolstoy is right. Happy families are all alike—they have short memories. Unhappy families dwell on their particular "slings and arrows" of the past.

Conversation-Starter with Family

I put this in the Human Idiosyn-Crazies™ section rather than the Amazing First Lines of Books section for this reason: Since we all have our Human Idiosyn-Crazies™, doesn't family harmony depend upon tolerance? But at what point can't we laugh these off or ignore  them? At what point must we deal with them? Is there a point that we should just accept them, and move on?

This kind of discussion can be geared to any age. Ask the younger kids what should be done about the cousin who hoards all the toys at Thanksgiving? Ask the older kids about gossipy or mean teens in the family. There are surely lots of issues to discuss, but keep in mind the goal of family harmony. After all, family feuds do not lead us to happiness. But tolerance, forgiveness, and short memories surely lead to happier, more peaceful lives.

Wait! Wait for Me!

I've always been out of it. What's the opposite of cutting edge? I guess maybe, dull center.

That would be me. At least, when it comes to technology—I'm definitely dull center. No, even that's too forward looking.

When I needed a new toaster, I searched mightily for one that did absolutely nothing but toast two pieces of ordinary bread. Nothing else! My TV, which I rarely watch, is from the 1990s. Yes, really. And why not? The toaster toasts. The TV shows shows.

But it's not only technology. Social media! Why must I be on time-sucking Facebook? But the worst is that the Devils keep inventing stuff that I don't need or want to know about. Pinterest, reddit, instagram, foursquare, etc...

Anyway, to further convince you of what an out-of-it nerd I am... *oh no*! Nerd is cool now (I think)! So that can't be me... I am an out-of-it something. The point is, I know nothing about pop culture.

But here is my dilemma. I don't want to be bothered with all this new stuff. On the other hand, and I never admitted this before... I really hate not knowing what's going on. There! I said it!

I want to know. I want to see. I want to understand. But it all happens so fast. And it takes so much time to get all this.

So I always feel like I need to run to catch up with the big kids. Wait! Wait for me!

Conversation-Starter with Teens

Teens will like this: Play a game with them where they name pop culture people or things and see if you know who or what they are. If you laugh, they will too.

When you're alone, you can Google all that you don't know, and then surprise them another day by starting a conversation with your new-found know-ledge.

Could you just tell me quick—What is Tumblr and who is Macklemore?

My Secret Gold

I sit in front of a bowl of gold. Deep gold with a greenish tint from the celery and dill.

Yes! It's the first official night of winter and I have made my world famous (a bit of hyperbole is part of the recipe) chicken soup.

Here's my recipe:

Put a lot in!

Yes, that's the whole thing. And I am rather insistent that this recipe not be tinkered with.

I am sure there are branches of cooks who believe in a high class, patrician-type broth. Not I!

I believe in a bowl of delicious stuff; a bowl so full of stuff that the broth can only peak around the sides of the bowl and pop up among the carrots.

I use the largest possible pot and put in lots of chicken, and onions, and rutabaga, and turnip, and parsnip, and carrots, and celery, and an even larger parcel of fresh dill. *Yum*! (And what fun to buy rutabaga, and turnip, and parsnip. It's the only time I get to buy those.) Once I've added my ingredients, I cook it for a long time. And then eat it.

That is my secret recipe.

You'll Notice that no new-fangled food processors are needed.

What kind of soup does everyone like? Plan to make a soup together next time everyone is home (maybe snowed in?). Ask the preschoolers, would you rather eat hot soup in the summer or the winter? Why? If you live in a

warm climate, do you eat much soup? Discuss whether it would be a good idea. How about cold soups? If you live in a cold climate, what other foods keep you warm? Yes, hot chocolate... but what else?

Just put the stuff in and cook it.

The other thing I do is this: I cook for multitudes, armies, legions. Since I don't cook often, when I do, I figure I might as well make a lot.

I see, in rereading what I've written here, that I am rather adamant, to the point of being a true believer, in the virtue of "a lot."

So... I have made my chicken soup with a lot of stuff in it. And I've made enough for an awful lot of people...

Hey! Wanna come over for some chicken soup? My bowl of gold?

The Refuge

They still want me to make a late appointment and be the last customer. I think they just want to make fun of the way my arms flail around.

What is it about hair salons that make them such special places? Places of relaxation. Places of easy conversation and laughter. Nowadays, many are unisex, but let's talk about the ones that are populated predominantly by women. Men, listen up—you may learn something.

Ah . Sigh. So restful. So friendly.

You talk to your hair stylist or nail technician about the details of your life, and the amazing thing is, that although you haven't seen them for weeks, they remember your angst about your child, your parent, your coworker, your weight, your wrinkles, your back, your bathroom renovation, and your roof repair. You're a two person book club. You're a two person movie critic. My hair stylist found me my last realtor. She now has her eyes and ears open for conference planners for my motivational speaking.

So back to the late appointment I was talking about. Once, after my late mani-pedi, the manicurists locked the door after the last patron (except me), turned the CDs up loud, and we all began to dance. It was a girl's night out!

And do you think you can get closer to heaven than soaking your feet in the bubbling warm water whilst reclining in the big chair?

Sometimes, soaking time is conducive to talking with the woman soaking next to you. I was having such an innocuous conversation and the two of us were laughing convivially, when she suddenly said, "I'm going to share my secret with you." Well now, that's enticing, isn't it? I listened most intently to her secret, but I am going to share with you only that it involved feminine lubrication.

My hair stylist and I have talked through all kinds of life events, hers and mine. From weddings, to deaths, to Thanksgiving dramas. Aging parents, difficult clients, and beautiful new babies.

One more word about heaven: facial.

Lying under warm blankets, lotions and potions patted upon your face, steam warming you from outside in, Indian music transporting you...

Oh! Sorry! I dozed off on my imaginary facial bed.

So, hey—you think this is an American phenomenon, or maybe one that only occurs in the well-off Western world?

Nope.

Recently, I was lucky to see the exhibit at the National Geographic Museum called <u>Women of Vision</u>. This was an exhibit of photos of women around the world, created by women photojournalists. A photographer named Lynn Johnson took a photo that was my impetus for this Noticing. The photo was of women in a hair salon in Zambia.

Lynn called the salon "a magical place." She said she felt "a lightness in that place." It was a true refuge from the demands of daily life for these women, just as it is for you and me. I bet that sometimes, the women in that Zambian salon even dance together.

I hope so.

Yoda

"Do or do not. There is no try."

This is a quote from one of my favorite philosophers—Yoda, the Grand Master Jedi.

"The road to hell is paved with good intentions." Another aphorism which I repeat to myself frequently. Yoda's declaration and this one are related. Both mean—just do it. (Although I really hate to quote the Nike slogan, it's true.)

Get off your butt and do it. Do not indulge your excuses. Do not cosset your fears. Do not blame your circumstances. Get up your gumption. Get up your energy. Get up and just do it!

By "you" and "your," I of course mean, "me," "my," and "mine."

I am the one who feels the need today to sit at Yoda's feet. But maybe you do too? Are you thinking of trying something new? "Do or do not. There is no try."

Although I have been a speaker for decades, and although I have been a writer my whole life, **now** is the time I want to ramp up. Now is the time I want to publish books and be a conference keynoter.

In the last paragraph, I said something twice that would bring on the disapproval of Yoda. Two times I said, "I want to." Yoda might say, "Margery, do or do not. There is no want."

So, for me, there is no "try." There is no "want to." There is

Conversation-Starter with Family

What does each person really want to accomplish or learn, but maybe is a little scared to get started? Start with the littlest ones. Would one of the kids really like to learn to ride a bike, swim, or ice skate, but is scared? Would one of the older kids like to learn a new sport? Do any of the teens have a career in mind, but it seems impossible? How can these dreams become more possible? Develop a plan with each member of the family. If something is expensive, how  could they earn some money? If something takes time, can something else that takes time be given up in exchange? And you, mom and dad, don't forget to make your own plan. It's never too late!

only the choice to "do or do not."

I must choose "do."

Are any of you out there sharing similar angst? Are you making a decision to move your life in a new direction? Will you join me at Yoda's feet and move forward with me as his protégés?

Or if you are not a nerd like me who believes in the wisdom of the Jedi Master, perhaps you would be interested in what

Henry David Thoreau had to say on the subject: "Go confidently in the direction of your dreams. Live the life you have imagined."

And when we begin again to cosset fear, let us remember Teddy Roosevelt and "dare mighty things."

"Far better it is to dare mighty things, to win glorious triumphs, even though checkered by failure, than to take rank with those poor spirits who neither enjoy much nor suffer much, because they live in the gray twilight that knows neither victory nor defeat."

So I raise my glass to you, that we may we know victory together!

To end this book, I give you:

IV.

One More
Amazing Noticing

The Edge of the Earth

I walked to the edge of the Earth.

It was dark and chilly and I was alone in the vastness of space and shore. The sea showered me with a cold mist, and its roaring was both alarming and comforting. Slowly, slowly, the earth began to subtly light.

I was overcome with awe. Golden light began to filter through black clouds. The sky separated from the sea and began to show its deepest blue through salmon, jasmine, and vermilion streaks. A fireball rose slowly from the edge of the vast ocean, and reflected back onto the waves.

Creation recurred. Light came from darkness. The sky separated from the sea. The land separated from the water. An awesome miracle took place, as it does every time our Earth turns round.

The sunrise out of the ocean is proof that there is no greater beauty than that which surrounds us day after day, month after month, year after year. There is no such thing as a hackneyed, trite, tiresome sunrise out of the ocean. The gift of natural beauty cannot get old.

The walk to the edge of the Earth in the chilly, dark morning was my birthday gift to myself. In my mind, I will be untying its bow and gasping at its majesty, for the rest of my life.

The Noticer's Guide to Living and Laughing

There is no end to the things we can Notice. This book is meant to get you started. Open your eyes, open your ears and all your senses, focus on what's right in front of you, and you will be truly living life. And I promise... you will laugh more.

You can keep up with my Noticings at www.DidYaNotice.com, and you can start conversations about them. Share your own Noticings, with your family, your friends, and your coworkers, and help them begin to Notice on their own.

Remember:

> *You don't have to change your routine to change your life.*
> *You just have to Notice what you see.*

–

Henry David Thoreau:
"It is not what you look at that matters; it is what you see."

Research on the Relationships between Mindfulness, Productivity, and Happiness

Now just in case you think this book is limited to all things interesting, clever, funny, insightful, witty, fascinating, and captivating; I want you to know that it is also about weighty, heavy stuff.

Noticing is mindfulness. Mindfulness leads to happiness and greater productivity. Harvard Business Review and Forbes have written about this. Research on happiness and productivity was even presented at the Royal Economic Society. See, there is good scientific evidence for Noticing, smiling, and appreciating life. Check out some of these:

- The August 12, 2014 edition of the *Proceedings of the National Academy of Sciences* (US) includes the results of experimentation about happiness led by neuroscientist Robb Rutledge of the Max Planck UCL Centre for Computational Psychiatry and Ageing Research. http://bit.ly/1tUy6ni Although my eyes followed the words of the original research article, I will report here the understandable summary presented in the August 10, 2014 Washington Post by science journalist Meeri Kim. Basically, the scientists found that if we are surprised by a happy event, we are happier than if we expected a happy event. Noticers! We can be surprised by things every day, if we just Notice them! Remember my

Noticing, "A Most Delightful Exclamation Point?" Let an "exclamation point fall upon your nose" and you will be happier by far! Research proves this.

- In the July-August 2014 *Harvard Business Review* contains the article, "Becoming a First-Class Noticer" by Max H. Bazerman. Bazerman quotes Warren Bennis, a pioneer of leadership studies, that the best leaders are "first-class noticers". Bazerman explains that this means "they pay close attention to what is happening around them. They see things that others miss...." Although this article is about noticing ethical lapses in an organization, it certainly points to the individual, corporate, and societal benefits of Noticing.

- The March, 2014 issue of *Harvard Business Review* is titled "Work vs Life." Harumph. That "vs" is not necessary. But there is a wonderful interview with Dr. Ellen Langer about the critical importance of mindfulness. I have responded to two of the articles in this HBR edition in my Huffington Post blog. http://huff.to/1qOhn4Q is about work-life balance. http://huff.to/1n5NKHy is about Dr. Langer's interview on mindfulness.

- The January-February, 2012 *Harvard Business Review* has a series of articles on "How Employee Well-Being Drives Profits." Researchers have found that happy employees are more productive. They have also found that the *small, everyday things in life* count the most in making us happy. Harvard psychology professor, Daniel Gilbert, notes: "Somebody who has a dozen mildly nice things happen each day is likely to be happier than somebody who has a single truly amazing thing happen... the small stuff matters."

Well... that sounds like... noticing amazing little things!

- Research presented at the Royal Economic Society's 2012 annual conference by Dr. Jan-Emmanuel de Neve and Professor Andrew Oswald demonstrated that happier people earn more. They report: "We find that human happiness has large and positive causal effects on productivity."

- Research psychologist, Sonja Lyubomirsky, notes that people "high in mindfulness—those who are mindfully attentive to the here and now and keenly aware of their surroundings are models of flourishing and positive mental health." In other words, they Notice!

- The Huffington Post has a section on mindfulness research which translates research findings for the layman, as well as a mindful leadership section.

- There are a couple of interesting articles in *Forbes* linking mindfulness to business success:

  - http://onforb.es/1jqedT7

  - http://onforb.es/1pRRmBG This article in *Forbes* is really interesting. Remember my Noticing about broccoli and all the repeating patterns in nature? These repeating patterns are called fractals. This article talks about the work of Pravir Malik who ties fractals to mindfulness in the workplace. He found that individuals becoming more mindful of their own patterns of emotion and behavior had a large impact on the functioning of the larger organization.

- Here is a website with lots of research on mindfulness: http://bit.ly/1rzviuc

Here are some of the companies that have instituted mindfulness training programs because they recognize the return on their investment of having employees who can focus: Google, Aetna, General Mills, Intel, Apple, Deutsche Bank, Procter & Gamble, Astra Zeneca.

About the Author

Margery Leveen Sher is the Founder and Chief Noticing Officer of The Did Ya Notice?™ Project. Margery is a writer, speaker, entrepreneur, and executive who has had a long consulting career working with corporations, government agencies, nonprofit organizations, and foundations.

Margery was a founder of a successful consulting firm. Her clients included multinational corporations as well as government agencies, including the White House. She has also founded numerous non-profit organizations and two charitable funds. In addition to *The Noticer's Guide to Living and Laughing*, she has a book on corporate child care, and a myriad of articles on various aspects of work-life balance. Her blog is www.DidYaNotice.com, and she also blogs for The Huffington Post.

Margery holds a Master's Degree in Developmental Psychology from Rutgers University.